CONTEMPORARY

PLAYWRIGHTS

BERTOLT BRECHT

The Plays

BY

RONALD HAYMAN

HEINEMANN · LONDON
BARNES & NOBLE · TOTOWA (N.J.)

Heinemann Educational Books Ltd
22 Bedford Square, London WC1B 3HH
London   Edinburgh   Melbourne   Auckland
Hong Kong   Singapore   Kuala Lumpur   New Delhi
Ibadan   Nairobi   Johannesburg
Kingston   Port of Spain

First published in Great Britain by
Heinemann Education Books Ltd 1984

First published in the U.S.A. 1984 by
Barnes & Noble Books
81 Adams Drive
Totowa, New Jersey, 07512

British Library Cataloguing in Publication Data
Hayman, Ronald
    Bertolt Brecht: the plays.-
    (Contemporary playwrights)
    1. Brecht, Bertolt—Criticism and interpretation.
    I. Title.   II. Series.
    832'.912   PT2603.R397Z/
    ISBN 0-435-18418-0

Library of Congress Cataloging in Publication Data
Hayman Ronald, 1932-
    Bertolt Brecht.
    1. Brecht, Bertolt 1898–1956—Criticism and interpretation.
    I. Title.
    PT2603.R397Z6667   1984   832'.912   84-9261
    ISBN 0-389-20492-7

Phototypesetting by Georgia Origination, Liverpool
Printed and bound in Great Britain by
Biddles Ltd., Guildford and King's Lynn

CONTENTS

A NOTE ON TRANSLATION AND SOURCES

The translations from the German are all my own, because I believe the advantages of retranslating outweigh the disadvantages, though these, undeniably, are considerable. There is no point in giving page references for English texts of Brecht's plays when my quotations do not match the published translations, and I have tried to provide accurate translations of titles (e.g. *Man Is Man*) rather than use the titles of published translations. It will be obvious that *Roundheads and Sharp-heads* is the same play as the one called *Round Heads and Pointed Heads* in the Collected Edition. The hardest title to translate is *Die Massnahme*, which is called *The Decision* in the Collected Edition and sometimes also as *The Measures Taken*. I call it *The Remedial Action*.

The reader who wants a comprehensive bibliography will find one in my biography of Brecht (Weidenfeld, 1983). In this book I have listed the most important works available in English, while the German section of the bibliography gives details of the books from which I have quoted. When a footnote gives only the German title of a work by Brecht, this usually means that it has not yet been translated into English. His *Arbeitsjournal*, for instance, should not be confused with *Diaries 1920–22*. But the *Autobiographische Aufzeichnungen (Autobiographical Sketches)* are included in this volume of diaries, while the *Kleines Organon (Little Organum)* is included in John Willett's anthology *Brecht on Theatre*.

CHRONOLOGY

1898 10 February	Eugen Berthold Brecht born in Augsburg, son of Berthold Friedrich Brecht (b. 1869) and Sophie (née Brezing, 1871).
September	Family moves to suburb of Klaucke.
1904	Brecht starts at Barfüsser Volksschule, a Protestant elementary school.
1908 September	Starts at the Augsburg Royal Bavarian Gymnasium.
1913	Co-founder and co-editor of school magazine *Die Ernte* (*The Harvest*) to which he contributes stories,
1914	followed by a short play *Die Bibel* (*The Bible*) and some poems.
August	Contributes patriotic poems and stories to the literary supplement of the local newspaper, the *Augsburger Neueste Nachrichten*. Also writes *Augsburger Kriegsbriefe* (*War Letters*) for an evening paper published in Munich and Augsburg.
1916	Almost expelled from school after an essay questioning the wisdom of wanting to die for the fatherland.
July	Uses name Bert Brecht to sign poem 'Das Lied von der Eisenbahntruppe von Fort Donald' ('Song of the Fort Donald Railwaymen') in the local literary supplement.
1917 March	Takes *Notabitür* (Emergency School Leaving Certificate).
April	Recruited as auxiliary war helper, he works as a clerk in a market garden.

October	Starts university studies in Munich. Joins seminar run by Artur Kutscher.
1918 March	Announces intention of writing a play about Villon, and sees performance of Hanns Johst's *Der Einsame* (*The Lonely One*).
April	At Kutscher's seminar Brecht attacks Johst's novel *Der Anfang* (*The Beginning*), and announces that he will write a counter-play to *Der Einsame*.
	Works on *Baal*.
October	Enlistment. Works in military hospital.
November	Probably elected as Soldatenrat – soldiers' representative.
1919 January	Brecht works on *Spartakus* – first version of *Trommeln in der Nacht* (*Drums in the Night*).
February	*Spartakus* finished.
July	Birth of Brecht's first child, an illegitimate son. The mother is Paula Banholzer.
October	Starts working as theatre critic for *Der Volkswille* (*The People's Will*). Falls under the spell of the comedian Karl Valentin.
1920 January–February	Collaborative work on *Baal* with Neher.
May	Death of mother.
June	Works on *Galgei* (later retitled *Mann ist Mann*).
1921 February	Begins affair with opera singer Marianne Zoff.
April	Proposes marriage to Paula.
August	Upton Sinclair's novel *Metropolis* inspires *Im Dickicht der Städte* (*In the Jungle of the Cities*).

1922	March	Abortively directs Arnolt Bronnen's play *Vatermord* (*Patricide*).
	June	Arrangements made for productions of *Trommeln* and *Dickicht*.
	October	Signs contract to work as a *Dramaturg* in Munich.
	November	Marries Marianne.
1923	March	Daughter Hanne born.
	Summer	Dramatizes Selma Lagerlöf's novel *Gösta Berling*, and works with Lion Feuchtwanger on adapting Marlowe's *Edward II*.
1924	January	Plans to settle in Berlin in the autumn as *Dramaturg* for Max Reinhardt's Deutsches Theater.
	February–March	Directs the adaptation of *Edward II* in Munich.
	July–August	Resumes work on *Galgei*.
	September	Relationship with Helene Weigel.
	October–November	Attends rehearsals of *Im Dickicht* at the Deutsches Theater and *Eduard II* at the Staatstheater.
	November	Weigel gives birth to their son Stefan.
1925	February–March	Works on text of *La Dame aux camélias* in Ferdinand Brückner's translation, changing it for Bernhard Reich's production starring Elisabeth Bergner.
	December	Finishes *Mann ist Mann*.
1926	January–February	Works with Elisabeth Hauptmann on revising *Baal*, and directs its first production for the Junge Bühne.
	April	Works on Marieluise Fleisser's play *Die Fusswaschung* (*The Foot-Washing*) which he retitles *Fegefeuer in Ingoldstadt*.
	June	Works on *Joe Fleischhacker*, a play about the wheat exchange in

	Chicago. By July, intent on understanding the forces that determined the market, be begins to read Karl Marx.
1927 January	*Bert Brechts Hauspostille (Domestic Breviary)* published.
Spring	Works with Kurt Weill on *Mahagonny*.
July–August	Works on *Fatzer* and on 'Augsburger Sonette'.
Autumn	Starts working for Piscator as member of dramaturgical collective.
November	Divorce from Marianne Zoff.
December	Working on dramatisation of Hašek's *Schweyk*.
1928 Spring	Elisabeth Hauptmann translates Gay's *The Beggar's Opera* for Brecht, who proposes it (March or April) to Ernst Joseph Aufricht.
June	Works on *Dreigroschenoper* in Le Lavandou with Weill, Lenya and Weigel.
August	Rehearsals.
1929 April	Marries Weigel. Publication of *Der Flug der Lindberghs* (radio version) in *Uhu*.
June	Works on *Happy End*.
1930 February–March	Rehearsals of *Mahagonny* opera in Leipzig.
Spring	Works on *Die Massnahme (The Remedial Action)*.
May–June	Works on *Die heilige Johanna der Schlachthöfe (St Joan of the Slaughterhouses)* and *Die Ausnahme und die Regel (The Exception and the Rule)*.
August	Submits *Die Beule (The Bruise)*, screenplay for *Dreigroschenoper*

	film. Nero Films rejects it but proceeds with the filming.
October	Birth of Barbara.
1931 January–February	Brecht directs *Mann ist Mann* in Berlin.
February	Première of *Dreigroschenoper* film.
August	Screenplay for the film *Kuhle Wampe* completed. Shooting begins.
Autumn	Adapts *Die Mutter* (*The Mother*) from Gorki.
November	Works on adapting Shakespeare's *Measure for Measure* to be produced by Gruppe Junge Schauspieler.
December	Quarrels with Weill during rehearsals for *Mahagonny* in Theater am Kurfürstendamm. Simultaneous rehearsals for *Die Mutter*.
Winter	Completes *Die heilige Johanna der Schlachthöfe*.
February	Police ban agitprop performances of *Die Mutter*. *Kuhle Wampe* film completed.
March	Film banned.
May	Travels to Moscow for première.
1933 February	In hospital for operation. Escapes to Prague with Weigel and Stefan when Reichstag is burnt.
May	To Paris for ballet *Die sieben Todsünden* (*The Seven Deadly Sins*).
June	Settles in Denmark.
August	Buys house in Skovsbostrand.
1934 February	Reworking *Dreigroschenoper* material as a novel.
March	Works on *Die Rundköpfe und die Spitzköpfe* (*The Roundheads and the Sharp-heads*).

	October–December	In London. Returns to Skovsbostrand late December.
1935	Spring	In Moscow.
	May	Sees performances by Chinese actor Mei Lan Fan.
	September	Negotiations over New York production of *The Mother* by Theatre Union.
	October	Goes to New York. Quarrels in rehearsal with company.
1936	July	Participates in international writers' congress in London.
	October	Involved in rehearsals for Copenhagen production of *Die Rundköpfe und die Spitzköpfe*.
	November	Copenhagen production of *Die sieben Todsünden* banned.
1937	March	Finishes first draft of *Generäle über Bilbao*, later retitled *Die Gewehre der Frau Carrar* (*Señora Carrar's Rifles*).
	August	Writes *Der Spitzel* (*The Spy*).
	September	To Paris for French production of *Dreigroschenoper*.
	October	Involved in Paris rehearsals for German language production of *Die Gewehre der Frau Carrar*.
		Returns to Skovsbostrand.
1938	January	Works on a novel about Julius Caesar.
	March	Works on scenes for *Furcht und Elend des Dritten Reiches* (*Fear and Suffering of the Third Reich*).
	May	In Paris for rehearsals of a German language sequence of scenes from it under the title 99%.
	November	Writes *Galileo*.
	December	Revises it on hearing the atom has been split.

1939	February	Works on *Der Messingkauf* (*The Purchase of Brass*).
	March	Works on *Der gute Mensch von Sezuan* (*The Good Woman of Setzuan*).
	May	Stays with sculptress Ninan Santesson on island of Lidingö, near Stockholm. Brecht's father dies.
	June	Completes the two one-act plays, *Dansen* and *Was kostet das Eisen?* (*What Price Iron?*).
	September	Puts *Der gute Mensch* aside. Begins *Mutter Courage*.
	November	Completes *Mutter Courage* and radio play *Das Verhör des Lukullus* (*The Trial of Lucullus*).
	December	Works on *Julius Caesar* novel.
1940	January	Writes story 'Der Augsburger Kreidekreis' (The Augsburg Chalk Circle') Writes *Esskultur* (*Culinary Culture*) a miniature detective novel.
	April	Sails with family and Margarete Steffin to Helsinki. Moves into a house in Tölö.
	May	Resumes work on *Der gute Mensch von Sezuan*.
	July	Invited by Hella Wuolijoki to stay (with family and Margarete Steffin) on Marlebäk, her estate in Kausala. Plans a play about a modern Joan of Arc.
	August–September	Converts a Hella Wuolijoki comedy, *The Sawdust Princess*, into *Herr Puntila und sein Knecht Matti* (*Herr Puntila and His Man Matti*).
	October	Starts *Flüchtlingsgespräche* (*Refugee Conversations*). Moves back to Helsinki.

1941	March–April	Writes *Der aufhaltsame Aufstieg des Arturo Ui* (*The Resistible Rise of Arturo Ui*).
	May	With Ruth Berlau, Margarete Steffin and family, he leaves for Moscow, where Margarete Steffin dies.
	June	Sails from Vladivostock.
	July	Arrives in Los Angeles. Settles in Santa Monica, Hollywood.
	November	Plans a version of Heywood's *A Woman Killed with Kindness* for Elisabeth Bergner.
1942	February	Registered as enemy alien.
	May	Plans production of *Furcht und Elend des Dritten Reiches* to be directed by Reinhardt.
	July–October	Works on screenplay for Fritz Lang. Brecht wants to call it *Trust the People*.
	August	Moves to a bigger house. Works on *Messingkauf*.
	October–January 1943	Works with Feuchtwanger on *Die Gesichte der Simone Machard* (*The Visions of Simone Machard*).
	November–December	Shooting of film, now titled *Hangmen Also Die*.
1943	February	Goes to New York. Stays with Berlau.
	March–May	Plans to collaborate with H.R. Hays on an adaptation of Webster's *The Duchess of Malfi* for Elisabeth Bergner. Commits himself to working with Piscator on a new version of *Schweyk*, but simultaneously plans a musical version with Kurt Weill.
	June	Completes *Simone Machard* and works on *Schweyk*.
	August	Peter Lorre puts up money to pay for

	a translation by Alfred Kreymbourg of Brecht's *Schweyk* script: Lorre is interested in playing the lead.
September	As Weill loses interest in the project, Brecht involves Eisler.
November	Brecht's son Frank killed, fighting in Russia.
1944 March	Louise Rainer arranges for Brecht to be commissioned to write a play for her on the Chalk Circle story.
June	Completes first draft of Chalk Circle play.
September	Birth and death of Brecht's and Ruth Berlau's son.
December	Starts work with Charles Laughton on a translation of *Galileo*.
1945 June	To New York, where an English-language production, *The Private Life of the Master Race* (*Furcht und Elend*) is rehearsing to open on 12 June.
December	Plans for a production of *Galileo* to be directed by Orson Welles.
1946 February	Goes to New York, where Berlau is in a mental hospital.
February–March	Works with Auden on *The Duchess of Malfi*.
March	Berlau discharged. Brecht looks after her. Spends over half the year on the East Coast.
Summer	Negotiations for Mike Todd to produce *Galileo*. Welles withdraws. Finally Brecht and Laughton settle on Joseph Losey.
August	Rehearsals begin for *Duchess of Malfi* directed by George Rylands, who reinstates virtually the whole of Webster's text.

October	After a week of performances in New York, Brecht takes over as director when Rylands returns to England.
December	Possibility emerges of doing some work in East Berlin.
1947 March	Edward T. Hambleton agrees to produce *Galileo*.
July	Opening of *Galileo*, scheduled for the 24th, postponed until the 31st, though the run has to end on 17 August.
October	In Washington, Brecht appears before the House Committee for Un-American Activities. Returns to New York and flies the next day (31 October) to Paris.
November	Flies to Switzerland. Weigel arrives with Barbara; Stefan is to stay in the US. Plans to work with Caspar Neher on an adaptation of *Antigone* in Chur, starring Weigel.
1948 January	Plans for a production of *Puntila* in Zürich.
	Rehearsals for *Antigone* begin.
February	Opening postponed to 15 February. Discussions with Gottfried von Einem, a director of the Salzburg Festival, who wants to involve Brecht in it.
July–August	Works on *Kleines Organon für das Theater*.
September	Arranges visa for a trip to East Berlin to direct a production of *Mutter Courage*.
October	Brecht and Weigel go to Salzburg and then, via Prague, to East Berlin. Official receptions for him.
November	Auditions for *Mutter Courage*. Erich Engel arrives to co-direct.

December	Negotiations with Wolfgang Langhoff for a studio theatre within the Deutsches Theater.
1949 January	Berliner Ensemble created.
February	Appointed as artistic director, Weigel starts preparatory work, while Brecht goes to Zürich.
March	Plans an adaptation of Nordahl Grieg's play about the Paris Commune.
April	Brecht negotiates for Austrian citizenship. Completes draft of *Tage der Commune* (*Days of the Commune*).
May	Arrangements for *Puntila* as new company's opening production.
November	New company's opening production in Berlin. Brecht simultaneously makes gestures of loyalty to the regime and applies for Austrian passport.
December	Commune play postponed; hasty work on adapting Lenz's *Der Hofmeister* (*The Tutor*).
1950 April	Brecht and Weigel granted Austrian citizenship.
October	Brecht agrees to write the *Salzburger Totentanz* for the Festival. Back in Berlin. Preparations for *Die Mutter*.
December	Rehearsals for *Die Mutter*. Works with Neher on Salzburg play.
1951 January	Preparations for production of *Das Verhör des Lukullus* (*The Trial of Lucullus*) at the opera house. Brecht goes into hospital for a check-up.
March	Performance of opera received unfavourably by Party leaders.

May	Works on adaptation of Shakespeare's *Coriolanus*.
June	Works on text for the *Herrnburger Bericht* (*Herrnburg Report*), a cantata.
October	Brecht awarded National Prize, first class. Revised version of opera, *Die Verurteilung des Lukullus*, (*The Condemnation of Lucullus*) is staged.
November–December	Works on *Coriolanus*.
1952 February	Decision to buy house in Büctow.
March–April	Brecht going regularly to *Urfaust* rehearsals.
July–August	In Bückow he works on *Coriolanus* and discusses *Katzgraben*, a play about collective farming, with its author, Erwin Strittmatter.
December	Works on *Coriolanus*.
1953 February–May	Rehearsals of *Katzgraben*, directed by Brecht.
April	Brecht and Weigel take part in Stanislavski congress.
May	Brecht proposes the formation of 'brigades' in the company. Brecht elected President of German PEN Club.
June	Rebellion of workers in East Berlin. Brecht declares his solidarity with the regime, also writing letters to *Neues Deutschland*.
Summer	Staying in Buckow most of the time, Brecht writes *Turandot* and the *Buckower Elegien*.
October	Rehearsals of *Katzgraben*. Moves into new house in Chausseestrasse, Berlin. In Vienna to direct final rehearsals of *Die Mutter* – Manfred Wekwerth has taken the early ones.

November	Rehearsals begin for *Der kaukasische Kreidekreis* (*The Caucasian Chalk Circle*).
1954 March	Berliner Ensemble moves into Theater am Schiffbauerdamm.
Spring	*Turandot* in rehearsal.
June	Elected Vice-President of East German Academy of Arts.
	Brecht visits Bruges, Amsterdam and Paris, where the Berliner Ensemble production of *Mutter Courage* is seen at the Théâtre des Nations.
December	Awarded International Stalin Peace Prize.
1955 March–April	Works on adaptation of Farquhar's *The Recruiting Officer*.
May	Goes to Moscow for award.
June	Back in Buckow, exhausted. To Paris, where the Berliner Ensemble production of *Kreidekreis* is presented.
December	Rehearsals begin for *Galileo*, which he is co-directing with Engel.
1956 Spring	Rehearsals of *Galileo*.
May	Brecht in hospital.
July–August	Gives advice to Wekwerth and Besson on production of *Die Tage der Commune*.
August	Directs a rehearsal of *Kreidekreis* which the company will bring to London.
14 August	Dies.

SELECT BIBLIOGRAPHY

1. WORKS BY BRECHT AVAILABLE IN ENGLISH.

    (a) *Collected Plays* ed. John Willett and Ralph Manheim

        1   *Baal, Drums in the Night, In the Jungle of Cities, The Life of Edward II of England, A Respectable Wedding, The Beggar, Driving Out a Devil, Lux in Tenebris, The Catch.*

        2.i   *Man equals Man, The Elephant Calf*

        2.ii *The Threepenny Opera*

        2.iii *The Rise and Fall of the City of Mahagonny* and *The Seven Deadly Sins*

        5.i   *Life of Galileo*

        5.ii *Mother Courage and her Children*

        6.ii *The Resistible Rise of Arturo Ui*

        7   *The Visions of Simone Machard, Schweyk in the Second World War, The Caucasian Chalk Circle, The Duchess of Malfi*

    (b) Individual plays

        Baal, trans. Peter Tegel

        The Caucasian Chalk Circle, trans. James and Tania Stern with W. H. Auden.

        The Days of the Commune, trans. Clive Barker and Arno Reinfrank.

        Drums in the Night, trans. John Willett,

        The Good Person of Szechwan, trans. John Willett.

        In the Jungle of Cities, trans. Gerhard Nellhaus.

        Life of Galileo, trans. John Willett.

        The Life of Galileo, trans. Howard Brenton (National Theatre version).

        Man equals Man and *The Elephant Calf*, trans. Gerhard Nellhaus.

        The Measures Taken and other Lehrstücke, various translators.

The Messingkauf Dialogues, trans. John Willett
The Mother, trans. Steve Gooch.
Mother Courage and her Children, trans. John Willett.
Mr Puntila and His Man Matti, trans. John Willett.
The Resistible Rise of Arturo Ui, trans. Ralph Manheim.
A Respectable Wedding and other one-act plays, various translators.
The Rise and Fall of the City of Mahagonny and *The Seven Deadly Sins*, trans. W. H. Auden and Chester Kallman.
St. Joan of the Stockyards, trans. Frank Jones.
The Threepenny Opera, trans. Ralph Manheim and John Willett.

(c) Poetry

Poems 1913–1956, ed John Willett and Ralph Manheim, also available in 3 volumes without the notes, 1913–28, 1929–38, 1938–56.

(d) Criticism

Brecht on Theatre, trans. and ed. John Willett.
The Messingkauf Dialogues, trans. John Willett.

(e) Fiction

Short Stories 1921–1946 ed. John Willett and Ralph Manheim.
(This and all the above are published by Eyre Methuen)
The Threepenny Novel, trans. Desmond I. Vesey (Penguin)

(f) Diaries

1920–22, trans. John Willett, London and New York, 1979.

2. BRECHT IN GERMAN
Gesammelte Werke (Werkausgabe) Frankfurt, 1967 (20 vols).

Arbeitsjournal, Frankfurt, 1973 (2 vols).
Briefe, Frankfurt, 1981 (3 vols).
Prosa, Frankfurt, 1980 (4 vols).
Versuche 1–15 Frankfurt, 1957–9.
Berliner Ensemble (ed.) *Theaterarbeit*, Dresden, undated.

3. BIOGRAPHICAL AND CRITICAL

Benjamin, Walter, trans. Anna Bostock, *Understanding Brecht*, London, 1973.
Demetz, Peter (ed.), *Brecht: A Collection of Critical Essays*, Englewood Cliffs, 1972.
Dickson, Keith, *Towards Utopia*, Oxford, 1978.
Esslin, Martin, *Brecht: A Choice of Evils*, London, 1959.
Ewen, Frederic, *Bertolt Brecht: His Life, His Art and His Times*, London, 1970.
Hayman, Ronald, *Brecht, A Biography*, London, 1983.
Needle, Jan, and Thomson, Peter, *Brecht*, Oxford, 1981.
Spalter, Max, *Brecht's Tradition*, Baltimore, 1967.
Völker, Klaus, trans. John Nowell, *Brecht: A Biography*, London, 1979.
Weber, Betty Nance and Heinen, Hubert (eds.), *Bertolt Brecht: Political Theory and Literary Practice*, Manchester 1980.
Willett, John, *The Theatre of Bertolt Brecht*, London, 1959.
Witt, Hubert (ed.) trans. John Peet, *Brecht as They Knew Him*, London, 1974.

Performances

| 29 September 1922 | *Trommeln in der Nacht* (*Drums in the Night*) at the Kammerspiele, Munich, directed by Otto Falckenberg, designed by Otto Reigbert, with Erwin Faber (Kragler). |
| 9 May 1923 | *Im Dickicht* (later called *Im Dickicht der Städte*, *In the Jungle of the Cities*) at the Residenz Theater, Munich, directed by Erich Engel, designed by Caspar Neher, with Erwin Faber (Garga), Otto Wernicke (Shlink). |

8 December 1923   *Baal* at the Altes Theater, Leipzig, directed by Alwin Kronacher, designed by Paul Thiersch, with Lothar Körner (Baal).

18 March 1924   *Leben Eduards des Zweiten von England* (*Life of Edward II of England*) at the Kammerspiele, Munich, directed by Brecht, designed by Neher, with Erwin Faber (Edward II).

14 February 1926   *Lebenslauf des Mannes Baal* (*Career of the Man Baal*) at the Deutsches Theater, Berlin (a matinee presented by the Junge Bühne) co-directed by Brecht and Oskar Homolka (Baal), with Paul Bildt (Ekart).

25 September 1926   *Mann ist Mann* (*Man Is Man*) premiered simultaneously at the Landestheater, Darmstadt, directed by Jacob Geis, designed by Neher, with Ernst Legal (Galy Gay), and in the small auditorium of the Städtische Theater, Düsseldorf, directed by Joseph Münch, designed by Harry Breuer, with Ewald Balser (Galy Gay).

11 December 1926   *Die Hochzeit* (*The Wedding*) at the Schauspielhaus, Frankfurt, directed by Melchior Vischer, designed by Ludwig Sievert.

17 July 1927   *Mahagonny* with music by Kurt Weill in the Stadttheater Baden-Baden, directed by Brecht, designed by Neher, with Lotte Lenya.

5 January 1928   *Mann ist Mann* at the Volksbühne, Berlin, directed by Erich Engel, designed by Neher, with Heinrich George (Galy Gay).

31 August 1928   *Die Dreigroschenoper* (*The Threepenny Opera*) with music by Weill at the Theater am Schiffbauerdamm, directed by Engel, designed by Neher, with Roma Bahn (Polly) and Harald Paulsen (Macheath).

July 1929   *Der Flug der Lindberghs* (later retitled *Der Ozeanflug, The Flight Across the Ocean*) with music by Paul Hindemith and Kurt Weill, directed on radio by Ernst Hardt, and then staged by Brecht on 27 July at the Stadthalle, Baden-Baden, conducted by Hermann Scherchen.

28 July 1929   *Die Badener Lehrstück vom Einverständnis* (*The Baden Didactic Play about Acquiescence*), with music by Hindemith, directed by Brecht, at the Stadthalle, Baden-Baden.

31 August 1929   *Happy End* with music by Weill at the Theater am Schiffbauerdamm, directed by Brecht and Engel, designed by Neher, with Carola Neher (Lilian), Helene Weigel (the Fly).

9 March 1930   *Aufstieg und Fall der Stadt Mahagonny* (*Rise and Fall of the City of Mahagonny*) with music by Weill at the Opernhaus, Leipzig, directed by Walther Brugmann, designed by Neher, conducted by Gustav Brecher, with Paul Beinert (Paul).

23 June 1930   *Der Jasager* (*The One Who Says Yes*) at the Zentralinstitut für Erziehung und Unterricht, Berlin, directed by Brecht and Weill, conducted by Kurt Drabek, with Otto Hopf (Teacher).

13 December 1930   *Die Massnahme* (*The Remedial Action*) with music by Hanns Eisler, at the Philharmonie, Berlin, directed by Slatan Dudow, conducted by Karl Rankl, with Helene Weigel and Ernst Busch.

6 February 1931   *Mann ist Mann* at the Staatstheater, Berlin, directed by Brecht, designed by Neher, with Peter Lorre (Galy Gay).

17 January 1932   *Die Mutter* (*The Mother*) with music by Eisler at the Theater am Schiffbauerdamm, directed by Emil Burri and Brecht, designed by Neher, with Weigel (Vlassova).

11 April 1932   Shortened version of *Die heilige Johanna der Schlachthöfe* (*St Joan of the Slaughterhouses*) broadcast on Radio Berlin, directed by Alfred Braun, with Carola Neher (Joan).

14 May 1932   *Kuhle Wampe* screenplay by Brecht and Ernst Ottwalt, premiered in Moscow, directed by Slatan Dudow, with Ernst Busch (Fritz), and Herta Thiele (Anni).

30 May 1932   premiered in Berlin at the Atrium cinema.

7 January 1933   *Anna-Anna ou les Sept péchés capitaux* (*Anna-Anna or the Seven Deadly Sins*) with music by Weill in French at the Théâtre des Champs-Elysées, Paris, staged by George Balanchine and Boris Kochno, designed by Neher, conducted by Maurice d'Abravanel, with Tilly Losch and Lotte Lenya.

Spring 1935   Scenes from *Die Rundköpfe und die Spitzköpfe* (*The Roundheads and the Sharp-heads*) at the Thälmann-Klub, Moscow, directed by Alexander Granach, with Alexander Granach and amateurs.

19 November 1935   *The Mother* (in English) translated by Paul Peters, with music by Hanns Eisler, at the Civic Repertory Theatre, New York, directed by Victor Wolfson, designed by Mordecai Gorelik.

4 November 1936   *Die Rundköpfe und die Spitzköpfe* (in Danish) at the Riddersalen Theatre, Copenhagen, directed by Per Knutzon, with Asbjorn Andersen (Iberin).

16 October 1937   *Die Gewehre der Frau Carrar* (*Señora Carrar's Rifles*) at the Salle Adyar, Paris, directed by Slatan Dudow, designed by Heinz Lohmar, with Weigel (Carrar).

1 May 1938   *Die Ausnahme und die Regel* (*The Exception and the Rule*) (in Hebrew) at a Kibbutz at Givat Chaim, Palestine, directed by Alfred Wolf.

21 May 1938   *Furcht und Elend des Dritten Reiches* (*Fear and Suffering of the Third Reich*) under the title 99% at the Salle d'Iéna, Paris, directed by Slatan Dudow, designed by Heinz Lohmar, with music by Paul Dessau, with Weigel.

August 1939	*Dansen* (*Dance*) (in Swedish, under the pseudonym John Kent). Two one-act plays *Was kostet das Eisen?* (*What Price Iron?*) and a variant on it at the Volkshochschule Tollare, Stockholm.
12 May 1940	*Das Verhör des Lukullus* (*The Trial of Lucullus*) broadcast by Radio Beromünster, Bern, Switzerland, directed by Ernst Bringolf.
19 April 1940	*Mutter Courage und ihre Kinder* (*Mother Courage and Her Children*) at the Schauspielhaus, Zürich, directed by Leopold Lindtberg, designed by Teo Otto, with music by Paul Burkhard, with Therese Giehse (Mother Courage).
5 January 1942	*Furcht und Elend des Dritten Reiches* at the Fraternal Clubhouse, New York, directed by Berthold Viertel, with Ludwig Roth.
4 February 1943	*Der gute Mensch von Sezuan* (*The Good Woman of Setzuan*) at the Schauspielhaus, Zürich, directed by Leonard Steckel, designed by Teo Otto with music by Huldreich Georg Früh, with Maria Becker (Shen Te).
26 March 1943	*Hangmen Also Die* premiered in Hollywood, directed by Fritz Lang, with music by Hanns Eisler, with Brian Donlevy.
9 September 1943	*Leben des Galilei* at the Schauspielhaus, Zürich, directed by Leonard Steckel, designed by Teo Otto, with music by Hanns Eisler, with Leonard Steckel (Galileo).
23 September 1946	John Webster's *The Duchess of Malfi* at the Shubert Theatre, Boston, directed by George Rylands, designed by Harry Bennett, with an overture by Benjamin Britten, with Elisabeth Bergner (Duchess).
8 December 1947	*Life of Galileo* (translated by Brecht and Charles Laughton) at the Experimental Theatre, New York, directed by Joseph Losey, designed by Robert Davison, with music by Hanns Eisler,

with Charles Laughton (Galileo).

15 February 1948   *Antigone* at the Stadttheater, Chur, Switzerland, directed by Brecht, designed by Neher, with Weigel (Antigone).

4 May 1948   *The Caucasian Chalk Circle* (English translation by Eric and Maja Bentley). Amateur production at the Nourse Little Theatre, Northfield, Minnesota, directed by Henry Goodman.

5 June 1948   *Herr Puntila und sein Knecht Matti* (*Herr Puntila and His Servant Matti*) at the Schauspielhaus, Zürich, directed by Kurt Hirschfeld, designed by Teo Otto, with Leonard Steckel (Puntila).

15 April 1950   *Der Hofmeister* (*The Tutor*) (adapted from the play by J. M. R. Lenz) at the Deutsches Theater, East Berlin, directed by Brecht, designed by Neher, with Hans Gaugler (Läuffer).

17 March 1951   *Das Verhör des Lukullus* (*The Trial of Lucullus*) at the Deutsche Staatsoper with music by Paul Dessau, directed by Wolf Völker, designed by Neher, conducted by Hermann Scherchen.

5 August 1951   *Herrnburger Bericht* (*Herrnburg Report*) at the Deutsches Theater, directed by Egon Monk, designed by Neher, music by Paul Dessau, conducted by Hans Sandig.

12 October 1951   *Die Verurteilung des Lukullus* (*The Condemnation of Lucullus*) at the Deutsche Staatsoper, with music by Paul Dessau, directed by Wolf Völker, designed by Neher, conducted by Hermann Scherchen.

7 October 1954   *Der kaukasische Kreidekreis* at the Theater am Schiffbauerdamm, designed by Karl von Appen with Angelika Hurwicz (Grusha).

BAAL

Brecht started *Baal* in the spring of 1918 when he was just twenty, very much under the influence of Villon, Rimbaud and Verlaine, and a long way from being a Marxist. After finishing it, he produced three other versions, one the next year, one in 1919, one in 1920–2 and one, called *Lebenslauf des Mannes Baal* (*Life Story of the Man Baal*), in 1926, the year he read *Das Kapital*.

He believed, throughout his writing career, that there should be a two-way traffic of influence between world and work. The first version reflects his life in Augsburg, where he had succeeded while still a schoolboy in making a local literary reputation, in building up a retinue of friends and admirers, and in seducing innumerable girls. He sang his poems to eclectic tunes of his own, accompanying himself on the guitar. His voice was high-pitched, raucous and untrained, but attractive: an extraordinary energy was both visible and audible in his performances. Caspar Neher, a close friend from his schooldays, later declared: 'Bert sings his songs, which never fail to make you feel better. Power, power, incredible power. Without any of that romantic nonsense, but tremendously evocative.'[1]

Brecht took his friends on nocturnal escapades. They sang, drank, made love. He could create around him the feeling of a non-stop party. The first version of *Baal* is a semi-autobiographical celebration of this kind of life, and of the power he had to bring it to his friends, as he brought them to it. According to one of them, Hans Otto Münsterer, the second version of *Baal* 'exerted a strong influence on our lives: in 1919 the whole of the early summer was permeated with Baal-like feelings towards the world. But the reverse was also true – the play, especially in this second and best version, itself contains a lot of the life we were leading . . . and in many passages of dialogue, the gulf between the historical actuality and historical exaggeration is none too wide.'[2]

1. Caspar Neher, *Diary*. Unpublished.
2. Hans Otto Münsterer, *Bertolt Brecht Erinnerungen aus den Jahren 1917–22*, Berlin, 1966, p. 109.

All this is positive, but the pressure which occasioned *Baal* was negative. In origin it was an anti-play, a play written to contradict *Der Einsame: ein Menschenuntergang (The Lonely One: Downfall of a Man)*, a romantic play by Hanns Johst about the nineteenth-century playwright Christian Dietrich Grabbe. As a student at the university in Munich, Brecht was attending a seminar conducted by Professor Artur Kutscher, a specialist in contemporary German literature. Johst's output had included a couple of Expressionist plays, *Der junge Mensch (The Young Man)* and *Stroh (Straw)*. Kutscher considered him to be as good a writer as Lenz or Büchner, and on 30 March 1918, the seminar discussed his third play, *Der Einsame*, which translated Grabbe's agonies and ecstasies into rapturous, over-explicit prose. Brecht was particularly irritated by the sequence in which the poet reviles his mother for the lechery that led to his birth as the son of a washerwoman and a postman. Johst had uncritically accepted the trite assumption that poets were soulful and self-sacrificial; Brecht, who had himself as a specimen for microscopic study, knew that they were no less sensual than other people. In a fit of creative pique, he told the seminar he was going to write an 'antithesis' to *Der Einsame*.

He started *Baal* by working through the printed text of Johst's play, substituting for each idealistic falsification a scene which corresponded more truthfully to human behaviour in general and to his own in particular. Baal is the anti-type to Johst's Grabbe, dedicated to satisfying his physical appetites, where Grabbe agonizes, orates, strikes spiritual poses. Many of Brecht's characters are named after Johst's: Ekart after Eckardt, Johannes after Hans, Anna – in later drafts she becomes Johanna – after Anna.

In the German theatre Expressionism had taken its character from the younger generation's resistance to the oppressive weight of paternalistic authoritarianism and to the brutalities of the First World War. The plays of Ernst Toller, Walter Hasenclever, Reinhard Sorge were often shrill, strident; only Wedekind, whose *Frühlings Erwachen (Spring Awakening)* was written in 1891 though not staged until 1906, managed to earth his plays accurately in reality without condoning the mismanagement of life that made the contemporary world what it was. Brecht greatly admired Wedekind, and like Lulu in his *Erdgeist (Earth Spirit*, written 1895) and *Pandoras Büchse*

(*Pandora's Box*, written 1904), Baal is a personification of libidinous desire, devoid of moral responsibility. 'When you've slept with her', he tells Johannes, who is in love with a virgin, 'perhaps she'll just be a heap of flesh, faceless.' And when Johannes rhapsodizes about his love for 'the sweetest of women', Baal answers: 'There's no lovelier pleasure than a young woman's body . . . When you embrace virginal hips, warm life pulses in your hands, and in the fear and bliss of the creature you become a god. In the dance through hell. Hupp! And whipped through paradise. Hupp! Hupp!' For Baal, as for the promiscuous Brecht, little depends on personality.

In choosing the name 'Baal', he was associating his *alter ego* both with a fertility god and with Verlaine: hanging on the wall in Brecht's room was a painting of the god by Caspar Neher, who had modelled it on photographs and drawings of the French poet. In the 1918 Weimar edition of Verlaine's collected poems he is described as looking (when under the influence of absinthe) 'more and more like Socrates or a faun'; in the 1918 draft of Brecht's play Baal is characterized as having 'the precise skull of Socrates and Verlaine'. The 1922 edition of the play contains a reproduction of Neher's Baal, while Verlaine's relationship with Rimbaud is paralleled in Baal's with Ekart. Until the quarrel which culminates in the murder of Ekart, the homosexual lovers are happily leading a peripatetic life.

Though the dialogue and the emotional intensity are Rimbaudesque, *Baal* is partly a play about Villon. In March 1918, before seeing *Der Einsame*, Brecht had told Neher: 'I want to write a play about François Villon, who was a murderer, highway robber and balladeer in the 15th century in Brittany.'[1] As a balladeer himself, contemptuous of bourgeois proprieties, Brecht could readily identify with the outlaw poet. The choice of Baal as a hero was partly dictated by anti-religious reaction against the ferocious Old Testament prophets who had denounced the ritual orgies that Phoenicians and Canaanites dedicated to their god. Brecht's ballads often kicked against religious repressiveness, and 'Die Legende der Dirne Evelyn Roe' ('The Legend of the Prostitute Evelyn Roe'), the eighteen-stanza ballad he incorporated into the first draft of *Baal*, tells the story of an innocent girl who asks the captain of a ship whether he will take her to

1. Letter to Caspar Neher, March 1918.

the Holy Land. She is allowed on board, but the men make her pay for the ride with her body, and when, in despair, she jumps overboard, she is turned away from heaven as being too sinful, and from hell as being too devout. The ballad is irrelevant to the main action of *Baal*, but relevant to the main theme because it deals with the consequences of indulging appetites. Baal's only principle is to ignore all principles and succumb to all fleshly temptations, regardless of repercussions. His lust for life is irrepressible, and he justifies himself by his talent for living at full throttle. When his energy begins to slacken, he dies, and no explanation is offered of what causes his death.

The laconic style of the writing is appropriate to the character and the subject-matter: neither Baal nor Brecht feels any need to explain. They are enjoying and celebrating surges of natural life which should be self-evident. The construction is episodic. Incidents are strung together – almost, apparently, at random. Baal is seen spurning the proffered patronage of patronizing burghers, singing his ballads at an inn used by lorry drivers, seducing the virgin that his friend Johannes loves, carrying on an affair with two under-aged sisters, casually seducing a virginal actress, being enraged by the abuse of birch trees nailed to the walls of houses on Corpus Christi Day, singing at a night-club, drunkenly playing practical jokes, talking amiably to a corpse in the forest, abandoning the girl he has impregnated, arriving with stolen champagne at a seedy bar on a windy night, tiring of love affairs, picking a quarrel with Ekart and, killing him, dying unrepentantly. In the first draft there are sequences in which he feels remorse and verges on repentance, but these are cut from the second.

Baal is a poetic play in which the poetry filters from language into character and action. As in a Shakespeare play, many arresting images are created, some verbally, some three-dimensionally. Sometimes the stage picture is eclipsed by the picture that the words create, as when Baal, with Sophie nestling against him under the trees on a spring night, tells her: 'Love tears the clothes from the body like a whirlpool and then, after a glimpse of heaven, one is buried naked under dead leaves.' The Rimbaudesque language scarcely ever fails to make a strong impact: even beggars, waitresses and woodcutters are highly articulate. But the stage picture is sometimes dominant, as when we see a corpse in the grass, surrounded by six or seven woodcutters, who are sitting on the ground leaning against a tree. Often sound effects intensify the atmosphere, as in a hut scene, when rain is audible. Sometimes the savage poetry in the action is inseparable from the verbal and visual poetry, as when a red-haired girl with a full figure emerges from a thicket of hazel shrubs, looking for Ekart whom she loves:

> BAAL: (*reaches slowly for her throat*): That's your throat? Do you know how they kill doves or wild ducks in the forest?
> THE GIRL: Jesus Maria! (*Struggles*): Leave me alone.
> BAAL: With those weak knees? You're dropping. You want to be taken between the willows. A man's a man. In that respect most of them are the same. (*Takes her in his arms.*)
> THE GIRL (*trembling*): Please let me go! Please!
> BAAL: A shameless quail! Over here! Saved by a desperate man! (*Grabs her arms and drags her into the bushes.*)

Johst's play strains to make Grabbe impressive; the twenty-year-old Brecht had enough self-confidence just to let his own energy, articulacy and zest for living overflow impressively into the character.

The brutality, the terseness, and the episodic construction may derive partly from Büchner, but in a dramatic literature which was poor in poetic drama, despite the *Sturm und Drang* vogue for imitating Shakespeare, *Baal* was a remarkable achievement.

DRUMS IN THE NIGHT

The Life Force pulses heroically through Baal; in Brecht's second play *Trommeln in der Nacht* (*Drums in the Night*), the hunger for life in Kragler, the main character, is made to look shabby. This is a prose play in which environment, atmosphere and characterization are as unpoetic as the language. The main choice Kragler has to make is between risking his life on the barricades during the Spartacist rebellion of January 1919, and going home to live in abject comfort with a girl who is pregnant, though not by him. Like Baal, Kragler is fortified by brash indifference to conventional morality, and like Brecht he enjoys springing surprises. Content that he will not have to sleep alone, he goes home.

Brecht's original intention was to call the play *Spartakus*. Led by Karl Liebknecht, who had been in prison until October 1918, and by the Polish revolutionary, Rosa Luxemburg, the Spartacus Union was the only one of the three main German Socialist parties to want revolution on the Soviet model. Negotiations to end the world war were well under way when, at the end of October, the naval high command tried to order the fleet into a final engagement with the British navy. The ensuing mutiny at Kiel triggered uprisings in Wilhelmshaven, Hamburg, Hanover and Cologne, while in the south, Kurt Eisner, a leader of the Independent Social Democrats (USPD), the party which Brecht probably joined, recruited enough support from demobilized soldiers and members of the Bavarian Peasants' League to capture the military headquarters in Munich. On 9 November, the day Eisner proclaimed a Bavarian republic, Karl Liebknecht, addressing the crowd outside the Berlin palace of the Kaiser who was about to abdicate, proclaimed a Socialist republic. On the same day, a council of People's Delegates assumed power. Brecht may have been one of those appointed as a *Soldatenrat* (soldiers' delegate).

The new chancellor, Prinz Max von Baden, resigned in favour of Friedrich Ebert, leader of the principal Socialist party, the SPD, but the government could control neither the leaderless bands of soldiers who were on the rampage nor the soldiers' and workers' councils. When a congress of councils met in Berlin on 16 December, the majority proved to be moderate and anti-Spartacist, but demagogues went on inciting riots and demonstrations. The abortive Spartacist rebellion began on 5 January 1919, when workers occupied the offices of the newspaper *Vorwärts* and the Wolff Telegraph Bureau.

Without having been to Berlin, Brecht set the action of his play against this background, so for information about events he was dependent on newspaper reports. 'The revolution, which had to serve as a background', he said, 'was of no more interest to me than Vesuvius is to a man who wants to cook a saucepan of soup on it.'[1]

The construction is more conventional than in *Baal*, and more of the action is set indoors. In the first of the five acts we meet the family of a girl, Anna, whose fiancé has been missing for four years. Her father, Karl Balicke, is encouraging her to marry another man, Friedrich Murk, formerly an errand-boy, but now making a lot of money, as Balicke is, thanks to the war. Before they all go off to celebrate the engagement at what was previously the Piccadilly Bar and is now the Café Vaterland, Kragler appears in the doorway, just back from Africa, where he was a prisoner of war. At the bar his ghost-like presence helps to take the pleasure out of the celebration. Murk is coarse and unromantic in his attitude towards Anna, the parents are bad-tempered, rumours are circulating about the Spartacists in the newspaper district, and at one point Murk shuffles in with a prostitute. Eventually, machine-gun fire is audible.

Brecht was confused about the date when the rebels occupied the newspaper offices. There is no extant text of the original version, written in the spring of 1919 and titled *Spartakus*, but in both the published text of 1922 and the 1953 revision for the first volume of Brecht's *Stücke* (*Plays*), the action is set in November 1918, though the events actually occurred in January 1919. It was not until Brecht's collected works were published posthumously in 1967 that the action was shifted to January 1919 by a note. The third act is set in a 'street leading to the slums' (1922) and in a 'street leading to the newspaper district' (1953), while the phrase which gives the play its revised title, 'drumming in the night', is suppressed in the 1953 version, where the

1. Klaus Völker, *Bertolt Brecht: Eine Biographie*, p. 38.

exchange: 'They're drumming quite loud.' 'Hell! In our district!' is replaced by 'Gunfire.' 'Hell! In the Friedrichstrasse.' In both versions the waiter, who has followed the Balickes' party out of the bar, complains that Kragler is 'running after every drum'. In both versions Anna leaves Murk to pursue Kragler – in 1922 to the slums, in 1953 to the newspaper district.

The fourth act is set in a small schnapps distillery, where the Spartacist landlord, Glubb, sings the 'Ballad of the Dead Soldier', which Brecht had written before starting on the play. Called up at the beginning of October 1918, when the war was virtually over, he had about three weeks in a barracks before being posted, inadequately trained, to an emergency military hospital, which had been set up in the playground of an Augsburg primary school. Most of the patients in the ward where he worked were suffering from venereal disease. His imagination was certainly fired, but this was probably due more to the stories he heard than to his direct experiences. The most important image he crystallized was of a dead soldier, exhumed, renovated by military doctors, blessed by the chaplain and sent to fight once again for the Kaiser:

> Two orderlies to hold him up
> Are summoned in great haste.
> Otherwise he'd flop in the mud
> And that would be a waste

The image of a moving corpse is seminal to the play: without it, Brecht might never have hit on the idea of Kragler's entrance in a muddy artillery uniform to interrupt the celebration at the end of Act One, and in Act Four, Augusta, the prostitute, says of him: 'He just feels like a corpse; he's survived himself.' Though there is much less verse than in *Baal*, there is some poetic resonance to the implication that the bourgeoisie will not be allowed to turn its back on the whole-sale slaughter in the trenches, and to carry on with its unimaginative life of squalid business deals and sordid sexuality.

In the fifth act shooting is going on all round them when Anna catches up with Kragler on a wooden bridge under a big red moon. He agrees to go with Glubb to the newspaper building, but only because he has lost his appetite for living. Anna encourages him to go, but confident of not losing her, he prefers to survive. He wants to go home. All the revolutionaries are doing is play-acting, and in using Kragler to strike a firm anti-romantic posture, Brecht is also rejecting the romantic conventions of theatrical illusionism. Finding a drum that has been left behind, Kragler beats on it, ironically proposing titles for the theatrical performance. 'The Half Spartacus or the Power of Love. Bloodbath in the Newspaper District or Everyman is the Best Man in his Skin.' He does not mind being called a swine, so long as he can stay alive. 'I'll put on a clean shirt, my skin's still intact, I'll take my jacket off, polish my boots. (*Laughs maliciously*.) Tomorrow morning the shouting will be over, but tomorrow morning I'll be lying in bed, procreating, so that I don't die out.' He staggers around the stage, finally throwing the drum at the moon, *'which was a lantern and the drum and the moon fall into the river, which is dry'*. Brecht's first strong anti-illusionistic gesture has developed organically out of the play's emotional substance.

FIVE ONE-ACT PLAYS

Like Shaw's plays, Brecht's rest on a mature dislike – fortified by work as a drama critic – of the way that other playwrights had written.

In October 1919, when he was twenty-one, he was invited to work as drama critic for *Der Volkswille*, the daily paper published by the USPD in Swabia and Neuburg. Reviewing a production of Schiller's *Don Carlos* at the Stadttheater, he used Upton Sinclair's novel *The Jungle* as a yardstick for testing seriousness. Once you had read about a workman who starved to death in the Chicago slaughterhouses, a man who had once believed in freedom but had been beaten with rubber truncheons, how could you become emotionally involved with the misdeeds of Schiller's ill-fated prince?

In Munich Brecht enjoyed himself less in the municipal theatre than in the Lachkeller, listening to Karl Valentin, a comedian who wrote his own sketches. 'Demonstrated here is the inadequacy of everything, including ourselves. If this man, one of the most penetrating spiritual forces of the period, brings vividly before our eyes the *complexity* of the interconnections between imperturbability, stupidity and *joie de vivre*, it's enough to make horses laugh and take deep inner note.'[1]

Though Brecht cannot fairly be accused of plagiarizing or even imitating Valentin in the five one-act plays he completed before the end of the year, he was obviously, to some extent, inspired by the comedian, while these comedies are completely different in style from either of his full-length plays. The one-acter which owes most to Valentin's inverted logic is *Lux in Tenebris*, though the theme is remote from any the comedian would have tackled. After being ejected from a brothel because he could not pay, a man pitches a tent on the other side of the road to hold lectures and exhibitions on the subject of venereal disease. Trade at the brothel soon begins to dwindle, but in consequence his audience dwindles too, and he ends up by going into partnership with the brothel madam.

In *Er treibt einen Teufel aus* (*He's Driving Out a Devil*), a village

1. Brecht, *Schriften zum Theater*, p. 161.

boy outwits a girl's vigilant parents, and seduces her. His technique is to make it look as though he is so confident of getting what he wants that her resistance merely amuses him. Brechtian comedy depends less on wit than on guile: he theatricalizes trickery, and the trickster is nearly always male. The female role is either to be the victim or to play a subordinate role. In *Der Fischzug* (*The Haul*) a drunken fisherman nets his wife and her lover when they are in his bed; he then enlists the help of six other fishermen to drop the guilty lovers into the sea.

Die Hochzeit, which was later retitled *Die Kleinburger Hochzeit* (*Petty Bourgeois Wedding*) anticipates Ionesco's technique of making furniture play a comically symbolic role in theatrical action. Alongside the pretensions to respectability, the home-made furniture gradually disintegrates.

Another of the one-act plays, *Der Bettler oder der tote Hund* (*The Beggar or the Dead Dog*), prefigures the surrealistic mixture of nonsense and logic that we find in Ionesco. An Emperor is in conversation with a beggar:

> BEGGAR: What Napoleon are you talking about?
> EMPEROR: The one who conquered half the world and then got so proud he had to have a fall.
> BEGGAR: Nobody could believe that except himself and the world. It's not true. Actually Napoleon was a man who rowed a rowing-boat and had such a thick head that all the others said 'We can't row because we haven't got room for our elbows.' When the boat sank, because they weren't rowing, he pumped his head full of air and floated, the only survivor, and because he was in shackles, he had to row on, but from down there he couldn't see where he was going and they were all drowned. So he shook his head over the world and because it was too heavy it fell off.

IN THE JUNGLE OF THE CITIES

Upton Sinclair's novel *The Jungle* had habituated Brecht to thinking of Chicago as the centre of the modern wilderness; and after *Drums in the Night* he was confident that he could set a play in a city he did not know. In August 1921 Sinclair's novel *Metropolis* alerted him to the dangers of treating work not as a means but an end.[1] Then in September, after asking himself what Kipling's contribution had been to 'the nation that "civilised" the world', he 'arrived at the epoch-making discovery that really no-one has yet described the big city as a jungle. Where are its heroes, its colonisers, its victims? The unfriendliness of the big city, its malevolent, stony consistency, its Babylonian linguistic confusion – in short its poetry hasn't been created yet.'[2] In his early poems the heroes had often been bands of adventurers or pirates on the high seas – refugees from the restrictive staleness of city life. Now Brecht tried to deal directly with urban evil in the play *Im Dickicht der Städte* (*In the Jungle of the Cities*). First he intended to title it *Freiheit* (*Freedom*) or *Die Feindseligen* (*The Enemies*). It was going to be 'a play about conflict, East-West, with subterranean implications. Scene: the back of beyond.'[3] Walking to the sound of falling chestnuts, and stopping to write dialogue on thin typing paper folded to fit his leather notebook, Brecht had the feeling that the dialogue was presenting itself to him as if he were writing from memory. Within three days he had written three and a half of the eleven scenes.[4]

Unlike the plays he wrote after his conversion to Marxism, this one was not to be didactic: 'If I present a conflict, it must be between the two men, not the two systems.'[5] What happens to the characters matters less than the way in which they are forced to become aware of their limitations, and then try to overcome them. This generates 'the personal atmosphere – in short the poetry. Resistance produces the comedy. Each of the contenders must be given every opportunity, but

1. *Tagebücher*, (Frankfurt 1974) 25 August 1921.
2. Ibid., 4 September 1921.
3. Ibid., 15 September.
4. Ibid., 18 September.
5. Ibid., 30 September.

one shouldn't want to prove anything.'[1]

In the struggle between the Malayan timber merchant. C. Shlink, and the penurious librarian, George Garga, the main point is that there is no point. Visits to variety theatres had nourished Brecht's anti-naturalistic inclinations, and in 1920 he had been thinking that if ever he had a theatre of his own, he would employ clowns to stroll about in the auditorium during the interval, chatting loudly about what was going to happen during the second half of the play. They could also talk during the action. Seeing Baal with Ekart, they would comment: 'He's in love with that filthy tramp.' Disliking the conventions of bourgeois theatre, Brecht would go on looking for ways to remodel them, emulating vaudeville or silent film comedy or sport. In boxing the two fighters have no reason for disliking each other, but each has a reason for fighting and for wanting to prove himself to be the better fighter. If Shlink and Garga have a motive for fighting, it is the desire to feel fully alive. 'I envied the happiness of animals,' wrote Rimbaud; 'I've observed animals,' says Shlink, minutes before he kills himself.

> Love, the warmth of another body, is our only grace in the darkness. But it's only the coupling of organs, it doesn't break through the barrier of language. Still, they couple to produce creatures who will stand by them in their comfortless isolation. And the generations look coldly into each other's eyes. If you stuff a ship so full of human bodies that it bursts, they'll be so lonely, they'll all freeze to death. Are you listening, Garga? Yes, the isolation is so extreme, you can't even have a fight. The forest. This is where humanity comes from. Hairy, with ape jaws, good animals who knew how to live. Everything was so easy. They just tore each other to pieces. I can see them clearly, with trembling flanks as they looked into the white of each other's eyes, bit into each other's throats, rolled on the ground, and the one who bled to death between the roots was the loser, and the one who trampled most other animals into the undergrowth, he was the winner.

This is a lament for the impossibility of living in the urban jungle at an equal pitch of animal intensity.

As in *Baal*, much of the language is Rimbaudesque, and the first

1. Loc. cit.

scene, which is set in the library, is full of direct quotations from
Rimbaud. When Brecht was most under his influence, he believed
that nothing mattered more than intensity. In 1920 he had written in
his diary: 'To be happy, function well, take time for being lazy, to be
committed, only one thing is needed: intensity . . . *Amor fati*. To do
everything with all one's body and soul . . . To be present at one's own
misfortune, dedicating oneself to it with every ounce of flesh. The
only time that's wasted . . . is time when you had nothing to tell yourself about things. Didn't yell, didn't cry out, didn't laugh, didn't
bare your teeth, didn't press your knuckles into your temple, didn't
even swim or take a catnap.'[1] Like Kragler, the young Brecht believed
in giving personal needs priority over political causes.

During the year before he started writing the play, his strongest
feelings had centred on the opera singer Marianne Zoff, who had
made him feel intensely jealous of her other lover. Brecht's hatred for
Recht was so violent that it was probably adulterated with elements of
love, but their relationship had nothing to do with personal character.
Brecht could therefore draw on it in portraying the clash between
Shlink and Garga. Though there is no sexual rivalry between his
characters, their conflict is like the one between Brecht and Recht in
being independent of personality and psychology. As a playwright
Brecht was unusual in being interested in neither. 'Concentrate
neither on people's behaviour,' ran the axiom he had formulated for
himself, 'nor on their opinions.'[2] The behaviour of Shlink and Garga
depends much less on Brecht's observation of individual behaviour
than on a distillation of the feelings that the Upton Sinclair novels had
precipitated about living in the urban jungle.

Though he was twenty-four years older, the Austrian playwright
Hugo von Hofmannstahl was quick to understand that Brecht was
fighting against the old idea of individuality, and in the prologue
Hofmannstahl wrote for the Austrian premier of *Baal*, he joined forces
with the young poet:

> Our age has not been redeemed. Do you know what it wants to
> be redeemed from? . . . The individual . . . Our age is groaning
> under the weight of this 16th century child fattened by the 19th
> to outsize dimensions . . . We are nameless forces. Spiritual

1. *Tagebücher*, 3 September 1920.
2. Ibid., 5 March 1921

potentialities. Individuality is an arabesque we have discarded.

The fight between Shlink and Garga begins in the library, when Shlink offers to buy an opinion from Garga, who immediately understands that he is being insulted and gradually comes to realize that if he is ever going to make a meaningful human contact, it will be with this adversary. 'Spiritual combat is as brutal as the battle between men', said Rimbaud. 'I'm not visualising faces', Brecht wrote, 'but facing visions. This is the only Expressionistic element! Not trends incorporated in individuals, but men as spiritual beings.'[1] Originally he wanted Garga to resemble Rimbaud: he was 'a German translation from the French into American,' while Shlink uses 'an appearance of passivity' to slash through Garga's ties to his environment, forcing him to fight 'a desperate war of liberation'.

Brecht's writing generates extraordinary theatrical tensions. Deftly, he makes a lot of the action contingent on the reactions of people who are only indirectly involved in the fight through their relationship with the two men. In the first scene, C. Maynes, the owner of the library, anxious because his property is being vandalized by Shlink's henchmen, puts pressure on Garga to sell his opinion. His girlfriend, Jane Larry, appears at the library in the company of another henchman, Baboon, a pimp, and Garga is told they have been in bed together. In the second scene, when he turns up at Shlink's office, Garga is surprised to find that his sister Mary is working there, doing the laundry. He has been earning too little to be generous either to Jane or to his parents, but Shlink, seeing that money will not make Garga capitulate, gratuitously presents him with the timber business. To counter this move, Garga sets about ruining the business: he commits fraud and gives away the house to the Salvation Army in return for permission to spit in the young preacher's face.

If it is homosexual love that is binding the antagonists together, as with Rimbaud and Verlaine, it never surfaces in the action, as it did between Baal and Ekart. The start of the motiveless fight is made theatrically believable; the problem that Brecht fails to solve is how to convince the audience that both men would fight to the death. He was borrowing from a Danish novel *Hjulet* (*The Wheel*) by J. V. Jensen, which had been published in a German translation earlier in

1. *Tagebücher*, 5 October 1921.

the year. Aiming at the 'spiritual rape' of a young journalist, a lay preacher tries to steal his views of life, separate him from his fiancée and frame him for a murder; but, during a boxing-match, the preacher feels love for the younger man. Brecht's borrowings from *The Wheel* are inadequately integrated, and his story-telling is incoherent: no audience could either digest the narrative information embedded in the cryptic dialogue, or know when Garga is quoting Rimbaud. Or why. Part of the trouble lies in the density of the material – too much unexplained action is packed into each of the brief scenes, and some of it is motivated, some not. Generally the inconsequential behaviour of Shlink and Garga is more convincing than that of the minor characters, who sometimes seem almost operatic in their violent changes of emotional tack. And after the seventh scene there is an awkward gap of three years to span the prison sentence that Garga has to serve.

As in *Baal*, the language is sinewy, and many of the verbal images are arresting, while some of the stage pictures are memorable. The penultimate scene is set in a deserted tent in the gravel pits of Lake Michigan at two o'clock in the morning. As the light grows stronger in the brush, the lynch mob closes in on Shlink, who is dying, having swallowed poison. He is alone with Mary, and he collapses just before the lynchers' knives cut openings in the tent, and the killers step through. Unafraid, Mary tells them to go away.

Earlier in the scene, in his last confrontation with Garga, Shlink has said that what he wanted was a fight, 'not of the flesh but the spirit'. Garga's retort is 'And the spirit, as you see, is nothing. It's not being the stronger that matters, it's staying alive.' The attitude is close to that of Kragler, and Brecht apparently endorses it, but if the action of the preceding scenes was intended to flesh out Shlink's efforts at launching spiritual offensives, it cannot be said to have succeeded. Brecht was already too much of a materialist to be interested in exploring the spiritual aspects of the conflict. In *Baal* the poetry in the prose dialogue and the ballads was at one with the poetry in the atmosphere and the action; in this play much of the dialogue rises to almost the same rhetorical level as the quotations from Rimbaud, but neither the atmosphere nor the action are at one with the dialogue. To support the verbal intensity it would have been necessary to generate greater theatrical tension.

THE LIFE OF EDWARD II OF ENGLAND

Centring on a destructive relationship between two male lovers, Marlowe's play *Edward II* has affinities with both *Baal* and *In the Jungle of the Cities*. Brecht decided to direct it before he decided to adapt it. After working for fifteen months as *Dramaturg* (script editor) at the Munich theatre, he was given an opportunity to direct a production, and, deciding against *Macbeth*, he chose the Marlowe play. His friend, the writer Lion Feuchtwanger, persuaded him not to use Walter Heymel's translation: why not collaborate on a new version? They consulted Heymel's text while working together, but what they arrived at was less a translation of Marlowe's play than an adaptation.

There is less iambic regularity in *Edward II* than in *Tamburlaine* or *Doctor Faustus*, but there is less still in the new version, which has rhythms that are strong but never smooth. In *Edward II* neither the King nor Gaveston is portrayed as noble or heroic, but Marlowe was writing a tragedy, and Brecht not only disliked hero-worship, he was already reacting strongly against the idea, which is nearly always implicit in tragedy, that events are inescapable. Edward becomes less tragic, while Gaveston is not merely 'base and obscure', as Marlowe's Lancaster describes him: Brecht makes him a butcher's son.

A ballad singer is introduced, and the narrative style moves towards what Brecht was later to call Epic, with suspense undercut by the summaries of events, provided (together with dates) at the beginning of the play and the beginning of each scene. This is the first appearance of the technique that was to be used in *Mother Courage*. The number of characters is cut down and the plot is simplified, though it was already too simple: in the first half of his play Marlowe unrealistically makes the dissident barons talk as if there is nothing they want from Edward except a guarantee that he will give up his favourite, and, after Gaveston's death, the persecution of Edward and the rise of Mortimer are treated in personal terms. Brecht makes no attempt to widen the social focus or to deal explicitly with the sufferings inflicted on the people by their selfishly feuding leaders, but, as Herbert Ihering said in his review, 'Unconsciously he lets the energy of the masses flow into his work'.[1] He had been decisively

1. Herbert Ihering, *Die zwanziger Jahre*, Berlin 1948.

influenced by the impression that there was a better relationship between performer and spectator at sporting events than in the theatre. Though the antagonists in *Edward II* are less motiveless than those in *In the Jungle of the Cities*, Brecht tries to adopt a viewpoint which is less that of the hero-worshipping poet or the objective chronicler than that of the spectator at a popular sport. It is not merely through the presence of the ballad-singer that a fairground atmosphere is introduced.

Brecht supplies more specific sexual and social detail than Marlowe, and he anatomizes the relationships more objectively. Marlowe tried not to idealize them, but succeeded only sporadically in focusing on emotional ambivalence in Edward and Gaveston. He also failed to differentiate clearly between activity and passivity, especially in Edward, who eventually surrenders his favourite, and ultimately surrenders his crown. Brecht's Edward is not only less noble: he is incapable of freeing himself from the pressures of his physical desires, and is incapable of renouncing either his favourite or his throne. Not that he can keep them by clinging to them, but he is forced into a more dramatic confrontation with his enemies.

Marlowe's Edward has no real conflict; Brecht's Edward faces in Mortimer a scholarly nihilist who is reluctant to enter the political arena, but having once entered, refuses to be held back by scrupulous regard for accepted values. Holinshed, the chronicler who was Marlowe's main source, depicted Edward's final internment in 'a chamber over a foul filthy dungeon full of dead carrion'; Brecht, unlike Marlowe, makes the audience accompany his character into the sewer, but it is here that the anti-heroic strain is strongly countered. From abject humiliation, Edward rises impressively to self-sufficiency:

> Upon me here, for seven hours, the dung
> Of London drips. But now this filth is hardening
> My limbs. Now they are hard
> As cedar wood. The stink of filth is making
> My greatness measureless.

When Lightborn, who is obviously a murderer, appears in the dungeon, Edward echoes Garga's hymn to extinction:

> Rain was good; fasting filled my belly. But best
> Of all was darkness.

MAN IS MAN

Brecht's previous plays had all been written quickly, even if they were substantially altered in revision, but after conceiving *Mann ist Mann* (*Man Is Man*) in 1918, at roughly the same time as the one-act farces, he let seven years elapse before completing the first draft. His original idea was that a dim-witted Augsburger, Josef Galgei, would be tricked into believing that he was a butter merchant called Pick, who had been missing. In the poem 'Das war der Burger Galgei' ('That was Citizen Galgei') Galgei dies without managing to establish his identity. He is buried with the name 'Pick' on his tombstone.

The premiss is that personality is unimportant. 'Do I have to waste time on the differences between one man and another?' Brecht had asked in his diary. 'Strain my eyes?'[1] In the winter of 1924–5 he arrived at a notion which was new to his work on the play, though, like so many of the values, the ideas and the phrases in his early work, it derived from Rimbaud, who had maintained that thinking was a passive process: 'It's misleading to say: "I think." One should say: "I am thought." '[2] Why not characterize Josef Galgei as a man who does not so much live as allow himself to *be lived*, a passive 'hunk of flesh, who proliferates inordinately, who, only because he has no centre, survives each transformation, just as water flows into any shape...'

> Here is the donkey who feels inclined to survive as a pig.
> The question is: is he living?
> He is lived.[3]

Brecht must have been aware of the connection between his subject-matter and the change of identity that was occurring when ordinary members of the German public, joining the Nazi party, put on brown shirts, but he cynically refused to adopt a disapproving stance. It was only later, as a Marxist trying to re-angle his early work,

---

1. *Arbeitsjournal*, 5 March 1921.
2. Letter from Rimbaud to Georges Izambard, 13 May 1871.
3. Note dated 21 May 1925. *Gesammelte Werke* Vol XV, p. 57.

that he would condemn the character's volatility, interpolating new lines to evidence disapproval:

> Unless we're careful not to let him out of sight
> He could become a killer overnight.

Brecht's personal assistant, Elisabeth Hauptmann, an enthusiast for Kipling, confirmed that when she met him in 1924, he was already familiar with Kipling's Soldiers Three, and he had used the epigraph about 'three friends that buried the fourth' in the 1921 version of *In the Jungle of the Cities*. But her English was much better than Brecht's, and with her on hand, it was easier to tap Kipling as a source. He shifted the action of the play from Augsburg to British India, changing the name Galgei into Galy Gay, and he made the man a fish-porter who turns into a soldier. This brings the transformation closer to Nazification than it would have been if Galgei had changed into a butter merchant, but in 1927, introducing a broadcast of the play, Brecht threw down a challenge to listeners. Perhaps they would object 'that it's regrettable a man should be duped like this and forced to give up his precious ego – all he possesses (so to speak); but it's not. It's quite a cheerful affair. For this Galy Gay emerges unscathed; he comes out on top. As a man who takes this attitude is bound to come out on top.'[1]

At this time Brecht was rather under the influence of the Behaviourism which was fashionable, and his anti-individualism predisposed him towards its mechanistic psychology. The traditional idea of personality was completely outmoded if individual consciousness consisted, like a machine, of components that could be rearranged. This is what the play sets out to prove:

> We'll take a man to pieces like a machine.
> And how much will he lose? Not a bean.

It seemed to Brecht that contemporary society was dominated not by the individual but by the collective and the mechanical. In the new environment a 'new human type' was evolving, and the new man was mendacious, optimistic, adaptable. Actually it is 'only seldom that he

1. *Schriften zum Theater*, p. 976.

can afford an opinion of his own'.[1] Brecht wanted Galy Gay to be taken as representative of the new human type; characterization and development correspond to Brecht's assumption that since life is so short, one must live it to the full, without wasting time on other people's sufferings. In relation to the social and political environment there is no need to do anything active: passive adjustment is enough.

During this phase of Brecht's thinking, Brechtian man lives at the opposite pole from Kafka's hunger-artist, who starves himself to death because he finds no pleasure in eating the food that is on offer. Brechtian man will tuck into any food he is given: nothing matters more than staying alive.

From Menander in the fourth century BC to Oscar Wilde in the 1890s, writers of comedy had made abundant use of identity confusion, but Brecht was probably the first to work from the premiss that differences between one personality and another were too trivial to matter. In style, too, he was breaking new ground, discovering that farce of the kind he had used in his one-act plays could be developed in a full-length comedy that makes serious statements about human nature and human behaviour. He had learned from Charlie Chaplin films that slapstick was compatible with poetry; the dialogue in *Man Is Man* also draws on the technique used in Chinese drama when characters present themselves to the audience. Galy Gay's opening speech cheerfully destroys any expectation that human behaviour will be presented realistically: 'Dear wife, I have decided today, in accordance with our income, to buy a fish. This would not be beyond the resources of a packer, who does not drink, smokes fairly seldom and has almost no passions. Do you think I should buy a big fish, or do you need a small one?' But the quaint solemnity also makes a claim on our attentiveness.

In choosing Chicago for the setting of *In the Jungle of the Cities*, Brecht had been opting for a locale that concentrated all the destructive forces of modern urbanization, while Garga's yearning for a carefree life in Tahiti reflected a pastoral desire on Brecht's part for a less oppressive environment. In choosing Kilkoa for the setting of *Man Is Man*, he was doing for the first time what he would do in several subsequent plays: selecting an unfamiliar and exotic environment as a

1. Ibid. pp. 976–8.

means of defamiliarizing the behaviour he wanted to portray –
making it harder for the audience to take it for granted. Long before
he coined the expression *Verfremdungseffekt* (alienation effect) he
was instinctively practising alienation.

Always a plagiarist – though never more ruthless than Shakespeare
– Brecht lifted his plot partly from a novel by his friend Alfred
Döblin, *Die drei Sprunge des Wang-lun* (*The Three Wells of Wang
Lun*) and partly from a story by Kipling, 'Krishna Mulvaney'.
Breaking into a temple, Wang Lun gets his pigtail stuck to tar on the
roof, and has to pull out his hair by the roots, leaving a bald spot;
Mulvaney (like Brecht's soldier Jeraiah Jip) is carried in a palanquin
into the temple, where he is taken to be a god. Anomalously, the
temple is a Tibetan pagoda, and Chinese people are praying in it.
Unable to extricate him, the three other soldiers, terrified of their
sergeant, who is known as the human typhoon, enlist the fish-porter
to take the place of the missing man. If a man is identical with his
social function, men must be interchangeable. The same point is
made about the sergeant, who is innocuous and powerless when he
appears in civilian clothes. His identity depends on his role, which
depends on his clothes. Later, in *The Life of Galileo*, Brecht will show
how a Pope's attitude can change as he is dressed in the Papal
vestments.

The scene in which the three friends gain power over Galy Gay is a
scene involving Brechtian guile, together with a comic style reminiscent of the one-act plays. Having coerced the unsuspecting fish-
porter into taking part in the illicit auction of what they tell him is an
army elephant – actually it is only an elephant head and a map spread
over a pole – they can convince him that a change of identity is his only
chance of escaping court-martial and execution.

The absurd trial scene which follows is the first of Brecht's many
trial scenes in which justice is not done and is seen not to be done.
There is no judge or jury, but Uriah combines these roles with that of
prosecuting counsel, leaving Galy Gay to defend himself, which he
can do only ineffectually, since facts and logic are feeble weapons
against nonsense and threats. Having testified that he was not present
when Galy Gay auctioned the elephant, he has to deny that he is Galy
Gay, but cannot deny having a moustache, and the auction, says

Uriah, was conducted by a man with a moustache. Galy Gay tries to change his identity again by asking Begbick to cut the moustache off, but Uriah is then able to produce the moustache, wrapped in a cloth, as evidence of a guilty conscience. He condemns the prisoner to be shot by a firing squad.

Though the style of the scene looks backwards to vaudeville and forwards to the theatre of Ionesco, Genet and Pinter, its substance derives from social and political reality. Most of Brecht's work on the first draft, *Galgei*, was done in July and August 1924. In March 1924 Adolf Hitler was on trial for his attempted *Putsch* of November 1923, together with nine others, including Ludendorff. The trial was front-page news in German newspapers. Hitler did not try to defend himself. 'I consider myself', he told the court, 'to be the best of Germans, who wanted the best for the German people.'[1] He was convicted of treason, but the court ignored the law that treasonable aliens should be deported. He was condemned to five years of imprisonment, but released after less than nine months. Sentences equally grotesque for their leniency were commonly passed on hooligans involved in right-wing movements: effectively, as Ronald Taylor has shown, a great deal of political power was vested in the judges whose values derived more from the Kaiser's Reich than from the Weimar Republic.[2] Unlike his English contemporaries, Brecht could never enjoy the comfortable feeling that lawcourts, though not infallible, were fundamentally fair. No English writer could have conceived the character of Azdak in *The Caucasian Chalk Circle*, the drunken clerk who becomes a better judge than any of the professionals: the idea is rooted in the experience of growing up in a country where justice was unavailable.

Certainly, the lawcourt situation has intrinsic theatrical advantages. It is usually full of suspense (and Brecht depended more on suspense than he admitted), while it forces the audience to think critically about the evidence adduced. It also tends to simplify issues on the principle that the truth must lie on one side or the other, with the plaintiff or with the defendant. But in many of Brecht's lawcourt scenes, it is justice itself that is, effectively, in the dock.

1. *Der Hitler-Prozess*, Munich, 1924, p. 28
2. Ronald Taylor, *Literature and Society in Germany 1918–45*, Bury St Edmunds, 1980

THE THREEPENNY OPERA and THE RISE AND FALL OF THE CITY OF MAHAGONNY

It was Elisabeth Hauptmann who drew Brecht's attention to John Gay and *The Beggar's Opera*, the 1728 ballad opera which had been successfully revived by Sir Nigel Playfair in 1920 at the Lyric Theatre, Hammersmith, where it ran for nearly 1500 performances. She made a German translation for Brecht, but he did not devote much attention to it until after he was introduced in March or April 1928 to a young actor, Ernst Josef Aufricht, who had taken a lease on the Theater am Schiffbauerdamm and was looking for a new play. Brecht first tried to interest him in one he had not yet finished about the Chicago wheat exchange, and it was only after Aufricht had revealed his lack of interest – they were in a restaurant and he signalled for the bill – that Brecht mentioned the ballad opera.

He had to work quickly. Aufricht wanted to reopen the theatre on his twenty-eighth birthday, 31 August; rehearsals would have to start at the beginning of the month. Putting the Chicago play aside, Brecht adapted Elisabeth Hauptmann's translation, interpolating material taken from Villon and Kipling, while shifting the action to the Victorian period. Gay's Captain Macheath was a highwayman; Brecht's Mack the Knife is a burglar and a stick-up man. Gay's Peachum was a receiver of stolen property; Brecht's Peachum organises a gang of beggars, equipping them to masquerade as disabled. Gay, whose social satire was only perfunctory, made the good-humoured point that lawyers and priests regard each other as cheats; Brecht saw an opportunity of demonstrating affinities between the middle classes and the criminal classes. Unlike Gay's Peachum, Brecht's has pretensions of bourgeois respectability. He can claim that his activities are not illegal, and can complain when the Chief of Police, Brown, fails to give him protection.

The second scene, the wedding in the stable, amusingly broaches the question of taste and manners. Macheath reprimands his gang for their lapses in both: they address his bride with too much familiarity,

24

fail to steal appropriate furniture and crockery for the occasion, fail to behave in keeping with the fashionable evening dress they put on. They start eating too soon and they tell dirty jokes. In exploiting the contrast between the violence that is habitual to them and the genteel behaviour they affect, Brecht was giving his middle-class audience a chance to enjoy its sense of superiority, but he was also suggesting that genteel clothes and manners often camouflage vicious behaviour.

The point is made in a different way when the police chief, or the sheriff, as Brecht anomalously calls him, turns out to be well disposed towards Mack. His appearance as a guest at the wedding scares the gang, who expect to be arrested, but Mack can safely admit that they have broken in to the stable and that everything Brown sees is stolen. The two men sing a duet, the Cannon Song, reminiscing about their experiences in India, where they served together in the British Army. Kipling is again the main source of Brecht's knowledge about army life there. And before Brown leaves, the dialogue establishes that he takes bribes from Mack and, in return, tips him off about police raids that are being planned.

Brecht was taking the view that traditional ethics were nothing more than a barricade to keep property and capital in the hands of those who already owned them. One of the premises for the play is Proudhon's maxim 'Property is theft', and the characterization of Peachum satirizes the people who find pretexts in the Bible for doing exactly what they want to do. In the original version of the first act, Peachum keeps a Bible next to the ledger on his desk, while hanging on the wall of his room are assorted moral texts, including 'Give and it shall be given unto you' and 'Close not thine ear to misery'. His first song is a morning hymn, and he searches in the Bible for useful lessons. A businessman, he maintains, needs both God and accountancy. And Macheath, after being taken to prison in the second act, and reducing Brown to tears with his reproachful silence, confides to the audience: 'That's a trick I learned from the Bible.' Inveterately anti-religious, Brecht was continuing the joke he had made by laying out his first collection of poems *Hauspostille* (*Domestic Breviary*) like a prayer-book, and recommending it for devotional use.

The most famous line in the whole show, 'Food comes first, and then morality', implies that virtuous behaviour is a luxury not everyone can afford. At root, the assumption is sentimental. Brecht takes it for granted that mankind is fundamentally good, that crime, evil, aggression are caused by social injustice, while the law, far from establishing moral norms, is merely a system for upholding the status quo. This sentimental optimism accords oddly with the suggestion that violence is as natural to us as it is to the shark, but we are clearly meant to agree with Peachum when, in the third act, he tells Brown: 'The Law was made entirely and exclusively for the exploitation of those who don't understand it or are disqualified by sheer poverty from obeying it. And anyone who wants to feed on this exploitation must observe the law strictly.'

Macheath's crimes of violence are treated very lightly in the text, while Kurt Weill's music helps to make the audience feel tolerant towards them. When they are listed by Polly in the first scene of the second act, they include two murders, over thirty burglaries, twenty-three hold-ups, several attempted murders, and a good deal of arson and perjury; but a catalogue like this does not have the effect of making the audience imagine any of the human detail, and, as Brecht understood, everything on stage is relative. If the other male characters are either more repulsive than Macheath, or subservient to him, or both, and if the female characters mostly find him glamorous, he will be attractive to the audience. And though there is little dramatic substantiation for his anti-moral moralizing, we are meant to find it not only amusing but convincing when he claims to be a member of a declining group of middle-class artisans, currently in the process of being swallowed up by big corporations backed by the banks. 'What's a jemmy compared to a share certificate? What's a bank robbery compared to the founding of a bank? What's murdering a man compared with being his employer?' Gay's paradoxes are not always dissimilar, but they are usually less barbed. The paradox of moral inversion had bred easily in the tradition of English comedy that runs from Shakespeare and Congreve to Wilde and Shaw, but literary German is not conducive to witticism of this kind. The playwrights who came closest to moral satire are not primarily comic – Lenz, Büchner, Wedekind.

From writing ballads and poems Brecht had gone on to writing a poetic play about a balladeer, and within ten years of *Baal*, he had adapted a ballad opera. In his zest for living and in his amoral ruth-lessness, Macheath has affinities with Baal (and with Brecht) but in theatrical style there is no straight line leading from *Baal* through the intervening plays to the production that made Brecht famous. After the premiere, Alfred Kerr, the critic who was Brecht's greatest detractor, was as enthusiastic as Herbert Ihering, his greatest champion. According to Kerr, it was a magnificent evening and a pioneering work.[1] Ihering welcomed the production as 'heralding a new world in which the barrier between tragedy and comedy is removed. This is a triumph of the open form.'[2] Productions followed in all the major European capitals, and in Paris even Jean-Paul Sartre and Simone de Beauvoir took to humming Weill's tunes and quoting Brecht's line 'Food comes first, and then morality.'

According to Arnolt Bronnen, the word 'Mahagonny', which was later to become almost synonymous with Berlin, first occurred to Brecht in 1923, after they had gone to hear Hitler speak at the Zirkus Krone. They had watched.

> the masses of brown-shirted petty-bourgeois, wooden figures with their falsely coloured red flag riddled with holes. The concept grew out of the word and developed alongside himself: what it meant during that summer was principally a lower-middle-class Utopia, that cynically mindless table-d'hôte state which was brewing out of anarchy and alcohol the most dangerous mixture for the witches' kettle of Europe.[3]

Brecht's *Hauspostille*, published in 1927, contains three Mahagonny songs, and the first of them punningly equates civil-ization with syphilis. The sailors set out for Mahagonny in the belief that

> Our ci-ci-ci-ci-civilis
> Will get cured there.

In Brecht's early poems, the adventurers who leave city life behind them in search of an alternative, mostly die frustrated. In 1926 Brecht had seen Charlie Chaplin's film *Gold Rush*, and the Mahagonny of

1. *Berliner Tageblatt*, 1 September 1928
2. *Berliner Börsen-Courier*, 1 September 1928
3. Arnolt Bronnen *Tage mit Brecht*, Darmstadt, 1976, p. 116

the poems is roughly equivalent to the American boom towns created by speculators. Influenced partly by direct knowledge of Berlin in the 1920s, and partly by indirect knowledge of the brutality described in the fiction of Jack London and Upton Sinclair, Brecht visualized a kind of decadent Utopia ruled by greed for money and cheap thrills.

Later in 1927, when Kurt Weill needed a text for the small-scale opera or cantata he had been commissioned to write for the Baden-Baden festival, Brecht suggested the Mahagonny songs; the first idea was to combine them with two poems which Elisabeth Hauptmann had written in English, 'Benares Song' and 'Alabama Song', and with an unpublished poem by Brecht, 'Gedicht über einen Toten' ('Poem on a Dead Man'). But, willingly lured into collaborating, Brecht reworked the material into an ironic eulogy of decadent consumerism. The 'Songspiel', which ran for about forty-five minutes, consisted of six songs with orchestral interludes. The sixth poem, 'Aber dieses ganze Mahagonny' is re-used in the full-scale opera *Aufstieg und Fall der Stadt Mahagonny* (*The Rise and Fall of the City of Mahagonny*) which Brecht and Weill wrote in 1927–9. (W. H. Auden's translation misses the point about syphilis.)

The libretto starts its story with the founding of the town by Leokadja Begbick, Willy the Bookkeeper and Trinity Moses, three criminals on the run. The site, chosen simply because their truck breaks down there, seems to be as good a place as any for founding a 'city of nets' to snare the unwary. Auden calls it 'Suckersville'. According to Begbick (a character who made her first appearance in *Man Is Man* as the unscrupulous canteen landlady who helps the soldiers to outwit Galy Gay), 'It's harder to get gold out of rivers than out of men.' Girls who want whisky, boys and money are soon settling in the town, and then malcontents from the big towns start flocking to 'the golden city' where liquor is cheap. Jim, Jake, Bill and Joe (renamed Paul, Jakob, Heinrich and Joseph when Weill objected that American names would suggest that the satire was directed against American values) have worked as woodcutters for seven years in wintry Alaska, and now they want to spend their hard-earned money on having fun. They rebel against the restrictions Bebick tries to enforce, and when it seems that Mahagonny is about to be destroyed by a hurricane, they introduce a new rule: 'nothing is forbidden'. Living riotously, Jake kills himself by over-eating, Joe is killed in the boxing ring by Trinity Moses and Jim gets ruined by staking all his money on his friend. For both the 'Songspiel' and the opera, the setting was a boxing ring – a scenic correlative to the theme of conflict between two men, which had been central to much of Brecht's work since *In the Jungle of the Cities*. Penniless, Jim cannot avoid the one crime which is unforgivable in Mahagonny: he cannot pay his bills. A corrupt court-room sequence (reminiscent of *Man Is Man*) reprises the theme of bribery, which had appeared in *The Threepenny Opera*. The judge is Begbick – Brechtian shorthand for the statement that justice is a tool in the hands of the dominant class. She acquits a murderer who bribes her, but since Jim's friends (like Macheath's) fail to bail him out, he is condemned to the electric chair.

DIDACTIC DRAMA

During a life rich in ironies, one of the strangest was that Brecht should achieve commercial success just after his conversion to Marxism, which made him shift his sights away from the commercial theatre.

His ambition was to find an appropriate form of theatre for contemporary subject-matter. After disregarding motivation in his *Jungle*, and looking at actions as pure phenomena, he thought he might go on 'to show characters without any features at all'.[1] It seemed to him that the events and developments reported in newspapers could not find their theatrical counterpart in plays like Ibsen's. 'Petroleum cannot be manipulated into five acts . . . fate is no longer an integral power, but more like fields of force to be observed as they send out currents in opposite directions.'[2] After reading *Das Kapital* in 1925, he felt that he at last had a key in his possession for the understanding of economic processes. He had developed his aversion to personality, individualism and psychology without Marxian theory, but now he felt: 'this Marx was the only audience I'd ever found for my plays . . . They provided him with illustrative material.'[3]

Friendship with the sociologist Fritz Sternberg, author of *Der Imperialismus*, encouraged Brecht to think of traditional literature as a superstructure that was helping to protect the interests of the oppressors. Excited at the enlightenment he was receiving, he came increasingly to regard theatre as an instrument for passing it on. In November 1927 he wrote that the '*radical transformation of the theatre*' must correspond to the 'radical transformation of our period's mentality': together with art and literature, theatre must form the *ideological superstructure* 'for a solid, practical reorganization of our way of living'.[4] Championing the idea of Epic Theatre – Aristotle had contrasted Epic with Dramatic, and more recently the phrase Epic Drama had been used by the playwright Alfons Pacquet and the director Erwin Piscator – Brecht claimed that it appealed less to the emotions than to the intellect. Here he was echoing Piscator,

1. *Schriften zum Theater*, Vol I, pp. 226–7.
2. p. 226.
3. Note printed in *Schriften zum Theater*.
4. ibid., pp. 184–6.

who maintained that drama 'should communicate not only excitement, enthusiasm, passion, but rather enlightenment, knowledge, understanding'.

There could have been no question of rejecting the opportunity offered by Aufricht, and the partnership with Kurt Weill was rewarding – not only in the material sense – for both men, but *The Threepenny Opera* interrupted the process that had begun with the reading of Marx. It was natural, after their success, that Brecht and Weill should want to go on working together, and, besides collaborating on their opera, *The Rise and Fall of the City of Mahagonny*, they worked on *Happy End*, a new musical from Aufricht at the Theater am Schiffbauerdamm. That Brecht failed to complete the script did not prevent the show from opening, but, partly because he was not fully committed to it, it flopped. His discomfort at working with Weill is apparent in the notes he wrote on *Mahagonny* in 1930, complaining that so long as words, music and production are intended to be integrated, the component parts will all be equally degraded, each acting merely as a foil to the others. The process of fusion involves the spectator, who also gets flung into the melting pot, becoming a passive (suffering) ingredient of the complete artwork.'[1] Going on in these notes to catalogue oppositions not only between 'dramatic opera' and 'epic opera', but between 'dramatic theatre' and 'epic theatre', Brecht argued that instead of implicating the audience in the action and eroding its capacity for action, epic theatre should stimulate its capacity for action, forcing it to take decisions, instead of merely providing it with sensations. In epic theatre narrative is more important than plot, he suggests, and each scene is there for its own sake, not for the sake of the rest. The assumption is not that human nature is unchangeable, but that it is in a state of flux. The spectator is brought face to face with the human reality that is presented as the object of an enquiry. The tendency is to show that ideas are determined by social circumstances, not social circumstances by ideas. The whole concept needs to be seen against the background of *die Neue Sachlichkeit*, the New Objectivity, the fashion in German culture that was tending towards utilitarian values. Brecht was trying to make theatre into something more useful.

Reacting against entertainment that served no purpose, he now

1. *Versuche* 2, p.103.

became interested in writing what he called *Lehrstücke* or didactic plays, expounding Marxist doctrine. At first he tried to divide his time between *Happy End* and these didactic plays. The first of them, written to be broadcast and then to be staged at the Baden-Baden Festival, was called *Der Flug der Lindberghs (Lindbergh's Flight)*. The American airman presents himself in the most desiccated way Brecht could contrive, announcing his name, age, family background and nationality before going on to catalogue his equipment and summarize the preparations he made for his solo flight across the Atlantic. The emphasis on his equipment and his mechanics tilts the emphasis away from his personal qualities, while the writing aims at a newspaperish factuality. The fifteen scenes have titles like 'Invitation to the American flyer to fly over the ocean', and 'Throughout the flight all the American newspapers speak constantly of Lindbergh's luck'. It is characteristic of Brecht's epic theatre to place each event, whether contemporary or from the remote past, in a historical perspective, but in this play fog, snow and sleep are expressionistically personified as enemies bent on frustrating the man. Conflict between the adventurous group of males and the malevolent forces of nature had featured in many of Brecht's early poems; now he was dramatizing it.

The text is written in blank verse, with an irregular metre, and it was scored, with Weill and Paul Hindemith setting alternate scenes, for tenor (Lindbergh), bass, baritone, contralto and chorus. The chorus sings the reports of commentators on Lindbergh's progress; Lindbergh sings of his determination to conquer what is primitive, and, after he has landed, the chorus praises his achievement. Later Brecht added a direction that the role of Lindbergh should be sung by the chorus. He felt proud of the step humanity had taken towards mastering its environment when air travel became possible, but he wanted the achievement to be credited to collective endeavour. The title was accordingly changed to *Der Ozeanflug (The Ocean Flight)*.

The next play, *Das Badener Lehrstück vom Einverständnis (The Baden Didactic Play about Acquiescence)*, was presented at the festival three days later, with the thematic question 'Whether Mankind helps Man' projected on a screen. The piece is written in eleven sections for a speaker, four soloists and a chorus, with a short film sequence and an interlude to be performed by three clowns. The chorus is divided into two parts to argue whether people help each other.

Four airmen are still alive after a crash. Are we prepared to help them? Brecht insists that until the world is changed – this vague phrase springs from devout Marxist faith in the possibility of changing all relationships – no help is to be expected. Death can be overcome, according to the chorus, only if men submit to historical necessity. The airmen must therefore be prepared to die. The pilot refuses to accept this. He does not want to lose his identity; he wants glory, fame. So he is excommunicated by Brecht – sent off the stage. The three mechanics, representatives of the working masses who remain anonymous, are willing to accept the austere edicts of the chorus and are therefore praised for acquiescing in the natural 'flow of things'. When the mechanics are asked 'Who are you?' they answer: 'We are nobody.' Many of the questions and answers suggest a religious catechism.

In the interlude a clown on stilts, Herr Schmitt, complains of pains. Apparently anxious to help him, two other clowns saw off first his feet and then his legs. They unscrew his left ear, saw off an arm, and then the upper part of his head, finally unscrewing the whole head. The idea may derive from an eccentric piece of clowning Brecht had seen in 1920 at a variety theatre, when a clown shot at the lights with a small pistol, and then hit himself on the head. When a huge bump swelled up, he sawed it off and ate it. But the sequence Brecht wrote for his didactic play is also a variant on the theme of dismantling the individual, which he had treated in *Man Is Man*. But at the Baden-Baden premiere the sawing of limbs and the spurting of blood (from a bladder concealed by the actor) upset the audience enough to cause a minor riot. Two of the clowns fled from the stage.

In his notes on the Lindbergh play, Brecht insisted that it had 'no value if you don't learn from it. It has no artistic value to justify a production which is not intended for teaching.'[1] By making the audience feel resistant, he wanted to provoke it into supplying an alternative. Later he would develop the idea that his didactic plays were not so much for instructing the audience as for instructing the performers. The impulse behind the writing was to enforce a severe discipline, and it was only on the performer that this could directly be imposed. He should not identify his own feelings with the emotional content of the text. He should pause at the end of each line. Performance was an exercise, a step towards the discipline which is necessary to freedom.

1. *Versuche* 1, p. 23.

As in *The Threepenny Opera*, one of Brecht's principal sources was the Bible: the didactic plays are Biblical both in language and in rhythm. Finding in Communism a surrogate religion with its own implicit promises of redemption and immortality, he was moralizing no less harshly than Calvin, and at the same time, he was thrown back on the Bible, which, since adolescence, had fired his imagination. His first play was called *Die Bibel*. It is six and a half pages long, and he published it in a school magazine when he was fifteen. Its main question is how to live in accordance with Biblical precepts. Besieged by Catholics, a Dutch Protestant city can be saved only by the sacrifice of one innocent individual. The son of the Mayor urges his sister to sacrifice herself, while her grandfather tries in vain to dissuade her: one soul, he argues, is worth more than a thousand bodies. The schoolboy Brecht had already been preoccupied with the problem of the one and the many. In the didactic play, the pilot is dedicated to the one, to himself – as Baal had been – but the mechanics, because they are willing to discard individual personality, are absolved by the chorus from death. They are to march 'with us'; joining the battle against oppression, they can survive – albeit impersonally – by helping to change the world.

The next of the didactic plays *Der Jasager* (*The One Who Says Yes*) was based on a fifteenth-century play *Taniko* (literally *The Hurling into the Valley*) by Zenchiku, translated into English by Arthur Waley, and, from his text, into German by Elisabeth Hauptmann. A teacher at a temple school is about to lead his senior pupils on a dangerous religious expedition across the mountains. A junior pupil, whose father is dead and whose mother is ill, begs to be taken with them so that he can pray for his mother. On the journey he becomes ill himself, and reluctantly the teacher submits to pressure from the other boys. They must conform to the ancient custom: if anyone falls ill on the journey, he has to be hurled to his death. The boy agrees.

The main change Brecht made to the Japanese original was to squeeze out the religious element. The expedition becomes scientific, and the boy's motivation is now to obtain medicine for his mother and advice from the physicians in the city beyond the mountains. Since there is no religious obligation to throw him into the valley, the climax is weaker, but to save the others from having to turn back, the boy acquiesces in his death, rather in the manner of the three mechanics in *The Baden Didactic Play*. The other boys kill reluctantly and affectionately: 'Lean your head on our arms. Just relax.'

After the 1930 premiere, one critic pointed to affinities between 'this yes-sayer and yes-men during the war'.[1] Afterwards, when the play was performed in various schools, Brecht asked teachers to hold discussions and report back to him on children's reactions. These were sharp enough to goad him into rewriting the play, introducing an epidemic in the village, so that the mother's illness is now one case among many, and the boy sacrifices himself to enable the expedition to go on and to obtain help against the epidemic. As in his schoolboy play, *The Bible*, Brecht was now weighing one life against many.

Brecht also wrote a second play, *Der Neinsager* (*The One Who Says No*), in which the boy refuses to be sacrificed. In this play there is no epidemic, and, as in *Taniko*, the only reason for wanting to throw the ailing boy into the valley is that ancient custom demands the death of anyone who falls ill on the journey. But this boy is no yes-man. Irreverently, but understandably, he challenges tradition. Why not start a new custom of abolishing old customs when they are evil?

The most important of these didactic plays is *Die Massnahme* (*The Remedial Action*), which is presented as a trial. Brecht liked the court-room situation, and again, as in *The Baden Didactic Play*, the judiciary role is played by a chorus representative of the Communist Party's accumulated wisdom. Four agitators have been sent on a mission to China; only three have returned. They killed their comrade, and they now have to explain their decision to the tribunal by re-enacting what happened. Intent on bypassing personal factors, Brecht makes the actors playing the agitators take turns at the role of the miscreant who was executed. This deprives him of a personality that is directly visible to the audience: his actions and his comments are presented as if in inverted commas.

Brecht's anti-individualism is also evident in the initiation sequence. Before setting out on their mission, the agitators have to repudiate their personal identity. Almost ritualistically they obliterate their features as they put on masks:

> You are no longer yourselves – you no longer Karl Schmitt from Berlin, you no longer Anna Kjersk from Kasau and you no longer Peter Sawitsch from Moscow, but all of you are nameless and

1. Frank Warschauer in *Die Weltbühne*, 8 July 1930.

motherless, blank leaves for the Revolution to write its orders on.

Like the three mechanics, they are content to become anonymous, and the rhythm of Brecht's prose indicates that he approves of their decision. It is also apparent that he is under the influence of Biblical rhythms and reiterations. Perhaps he is also trying to introduce in the audience a religious sense of duty:

> Whoever fights for Communism must be able to fight and not to fight, to tell the truth and not to tell the truth, to serve and refuse to serve, keep promises and not keep promises, take risks and avoid risks, be recognisable and unrecognisable. Whoever fights for Communism has of all virtues only one: that he fights for Communism.

Translated into English, this is strangely reminiscent of T. S. Eliot and of Thomas à Becket's acquiescence to martyrdom in *Murder in the Cathedral*, which was written five years later.

As in *The One Who Says Yes*, the executioners deal affectionately with their victim. Brecht uses the same sentence: 'Lay your head on our arms.' The young comrade has to die because he has proved incapable of subordinating his emotions to his intellect; he was therefore harming the Party he was trying to serve. Unable to watch passively while coolies were whipped for slipping in the mud, he tried to help them. He should have waited for them to rebel. Instead of allowing an innocent man to be arrested for distributing revolutionary pamphlets, he attacked a policeman, which drew attention to his comrades and to himself. He was unable to put on a diplomatic show of friendliness towards a repulsive capitalist who might have been helpful to the Party. Generally he gave in to his impulses and failed to preserve his anonymity.

Communist discipline may have appealed to Brecht for some of the same reasons that Anglo-Catholic discipline appealed to Eliot. Temperamentally the two men could scarcely have been more dissimilar, but they were both anti-individualists. Any austere discipline seems to offer an escape from the self, and appeals to those who dislike self-assertion both in themselves and in others. *Baal* had been a hymn to self-assertion; Brecht was now dedicating his work to self-denial. (In his private life he was inconsistent: austere in his working discipline and in his dress, but self-indulgent with sexual relationships.) To make the climax of this play less brutal, he added a scene in which the young comrade consents to die. When he takes the mask off, his face is seen to be different from when he put it on. Devotion to the cause has made him a better man. But he still has to die.

The play was written when Hitler was winning himself millions of supporters by appealing to the German people's irrational pleasure in the idea of self-sacrifice. As J. P. Stern has shown, 'sacrifice' is one of the most frequently reiterated keywords in Hitler's speeches. Brecht was not immune to the sinister glamour of the notion, but he was unaware of the Fascistic elements in his cult of discipline and of acquiescence to something dressed up as the collective will. His use of the chorus begs the crucial question of whether Communist doctrine and Party policy correspond to the will of the majority.

Die Ausnahme und die Regel (*The Exception and the Rule*, 1930) is another attempt to prove that there can be no justice in a capitalist society: that judicial processes are inevitably biased in favour of the dominant class. The main relationship in the first half of the play is between a merchant (bourgeois, malevolent) and a coolie (over-flowing with goodwill, oblivious of maltreatment). The action is set in Mongolia, and, shortly before a dangerous journey across a desert, the merchant dismisses the guide, whom he suspects of being too friendly with the coolie. In consequence the coolie, who is carrying all the merchant's baggage, keeps getting lost, but his energy, like his goodwill, seems inexhaustible. He has better reason than his exploiter to feel exhausted, but he offers to share his drinking bottle with the merchant (who has more water than he is admitting). Nervously mis-interpreting the coolie's gesture in approaching with a raised bottle, the merchant shoots him dead. This is distressing for the audience if the actor playing the coolie has succeeded in engaging sympathy.

In the law-court scene which ensues, Brecht goes on using his flair for making an audience tingle with indignation at the miscarriage of justice. In a parable he wrote for a school magazine when he was sixteen, Brecht showed a judge deciding in favour of four thieves for fear that if the verdict went against them they would cause trouble in the district. In *The Exception and the Rule* the verdict goes against the coolie's penurious widow. The rule is that the victim has good reason to attack his oppressor; how could the merchant have known that this man was exceptional?

ST JOAN OF THE SLAUGHTERHOUSES

In *Die heilige Johanna der Schlachthöfe* (*St Joan of the Slaughter-houses*) Brecht made his first attempt to combine the austere didacticism of these six short pieces with the entertainment appeal necessary to a play that will fill an evening in the theatre. But the contrast between *St Joan of the Slaughterhouses* and *The Threepenny Opera* cannot be explained simply as the result of Brecht's conversion to Marxism. The conversion was itself the result of trying to write a particular kind of play, more relevant than Ibsen's or Chekhov's to the main processes at work in modern industrialism. Though G. F. Hartlaub's phrase *die Neue Sachlichkeit*, (by which he meant 'the new realism with a socialist flavour') became fashionable, it denoted not a coherent movement but a general hostility to Expressionism, subjectivism, the bourgeoisie and current artistic trends. The drift was towards the objective and the impersonal, the functional and the streamlined, towards mass production and interchangeability. Brecht wanted a theatre in which the sufferings of the individual would be replaced, as subject matter, by collective issues, economic pressures, industrial relations, the movement of prices. At the end of 1926 he was trying to work on a play about the wheat exchange in Chicago, and it was while struggling to understand how it functioned that he started to read Marx. In 1929 tremors from the Wall Street Crash were felt in Berlin, where unemployment worsened, and, determined to unearth the causes of this collective suffering, Brecht worked abortively at a play called *Der Brotladen* (*The Bread Shop*), making it a premiss that hunger, poverty and degradation were the sources of all human suffering and all wrongdoing. This idea had been latent in *The Threepenny Opera*, and it surfaces in *St Joan of the Slaughterhouses*.

To Piscator it had seemed that the best way to politicize the theatre was by restructuring theatrical space to make a new kind of visual assault on the audience. Less concerned with architectural factors and visual impact, Brecht was generally less unconventional in his reliance on actors and words. But the modern historical play had to be quite

38

unlike the Shakespearian historical play, and in 1930 he was already aware that the gap between the two could be exploited ironically: 'I am going to let these 'heroes' speak in Shakespearian verse. This verse form rightfully belongs to them for the enterprises of the dealers and brokers are no less consequential – a matter of life and death for tens of thousands – than the battles of generals in Shakespearian wars.'[1] Like Tom Stoppard, who in juxtaposing two kinds of language in *Rosencrantz and Guildenstern Are Dead* is juxtaposing two sets of values, Brecht was inviting the audience to look critically at both. Blank verse rhythms we associate with heroic action are applied to prosaic commercial transactions or to a tycoon's profession of contrition about butchery.

> Do you remember, Cridle, how some days ago –
> We were wandering through the stockyard, it was evening –
> We stood before our new packing machine?
> Remember, Cridle, think of that great bull
> Who blond and big and dull looked up to heaven
> As he was killed: to me it was as though
> I died with him. Oh, Cridle, oh, our business
> Is a bloody one.

The parodic comedy is a form of alienation effect. First the actor has to stand outside the character, questioning the authenticity of his remorse. Is the tycoon deluding himself or deluding Cridle? Or both? Then the audience has to respond to the irony by looking at the tycoon in a Shakespearian perspective.

In 1927 Brecht had spoken scathingly about Bernard Shaw's commitment to socialism,[2] but *St Joan of the Slaughterhouses* is indebted both to Shaw's Salvation Army play *Major Barbara* (1905) and to his *St Joan* (1924). Brecht is making a Shavian point when he tries to show that the Salvation Army is an instrument which the capitalists use to ensure the survival of their system. Andrew Undershaft, the millionaire in *Major Barbara*, explains that you have to choose money and gunpowder in preference to 'honour, justice, truth, love, mercy and so forth . . . for without enough of both, you cannot afford the others.' This is essentially the same point that

1. Brecht quoted by Bernhard Reich, *Im Wettlauf mit der Zeit*, Berlin, 1970.
2. Hans Mayer, *Bertolt Brecht und die Tradition*, Pfullingen, 1961.

Brecht made – phrasing it more memorably – in *The Threepenny Opera*: 'Food comes first and then morality.' And in *St Joan of the Slaughterhouses* the idea is developed at some length. Wanting to prove that the lower orders of society are evil, Pierpont Mauler arranges for Johanna to be taken on a tour of the slaughterhouses, but the only dishonesty she encounters is the direct result of deprivation, so it is the employers who are responsible for it. As Brecht had noted when working on *The Bread Shop*, 'Our re-working of what is, classically speaking, tragic, must always refer back to the Bread Shop.' The evil must be shown to reside not in human nature or in fate, but in an economic situation which can be altered if only the energies of the workers are channelled into the class war.

As with *In the Jungle of the Cities*, Brecht's Chicago is based on what he had read in the novels of Upton Sinclair, and one of the starting points for *St Joan of the Slaughterhouses* is outrage at the possibility that a stockyard worker could fall into a boiling vat and be made into lard. Sinclair had also written (in *The Money Changers*) about the central role played by the stock exchanges in industrial activity, and, without quite understanding this, Brecht took the point up, making Mauler, when manipulating the local meat market, depend on information received from New York in a series of telegrams. Naturally the play cannot unmask the faceless men who send the telegrams; the audience's antipathy is conducted not towards them but towards Mauler, who appears to have all the Chicago meatworkers in his power. Prices go up or down according to the initiatives he takes, and the quantity of work available depends on prices. Brecht could have chosen to characterize him as motivated exclusively by greed for profit, like so many stereotyped capitalists in plays by Socialists. Mauler is more interesting but more temperamental: more convincing as an individual, but less representative of the economic forces Brecht is trying to drag into theatrical tangibility.

Piscator's solution to the problem was depersonalization. Using detached narrators or commentators to cite facts, using cinematic projection of dates, statistics, newspaper headlines, using masks to distort the actor or cut-outs of George Grosz caricatures to replace him, or giant projections of photographs to dwarf him, while bringing off elaborate (and sometimes distracting) feats of theatrical engineering,

Piscator was not primarily dependent on words spoken by individuals. Brecht was no less eager to focus on the collective, to show that history had its effect not merely on princes and politicians but on the anonymous mass of artisans, factory workers, servants. In the didactic plays he approximates more closely to the techniques of the Expressionists, using anonymity and the chorus, but in his full-length plays he works through individual characters. This often involves loading too much historical weight on the initiatives they take or fail to take. In this play the defeat of the general strike is implausibly contingent on the failure of one woman – Johanna – to deliver a letter.

Like two subsequent plays by Brecht, *Die Mutter* (*The Mother*) and *Die Gewehre der Frau Carrar* (*Señora Carrar's Rifles*), *St Joan of the Slaughterhouses* centres on a woman's conversion. Pelagea Vlassova, (the mother in the adaptation from Gorki) Señora Carrar and Johanna all begin by deploring violence. As a Christian, Johanna condemns the Marxist creed of embattlement. But observation of other people's behaviour – as represented in the action – shifts her inexorably towards the view that the end can justify the means, and that if social justice is to be achieved, bloodshed is unavoidable.

> Only force can help, where force prevails, and
> Only human beings help, where human beings are.

Here the blank verse and the rhetorical wording add to the persuasiveness. In the final scene she tries to declare her new-found faith in violence, but the vociferous capitalists and Salvationists make her inaudible. Because she has helped to maintain the status quo, they can afford to canonize her, but not to let her subversive ideas be heard.

THE MOTHER

Brecht's adaptation of Maxim Gorki's novel *Mother* (1907) is like *St Joan of the Slaughterhouses* in coupling the evangelistic fervour of the didactic pieces with the entertainment necessary to a full-scale play, and in centring on the conversion of a peace-loving woman to militant radicalism. Like Johanna, Pelagea Vlassova starts out from a position of religious piety, but less is made of this than in the novel. A convert himself, Brecht was eager to share the fruits of enlightenment, and in both plays the audience is invited to profit from what the heroine learns by experience. (Using female figures in a central role, Brecht was less inclined than with males to anti-heroic exposure of the clay feet.) No question of holding back now, as when writing *In the Jungle of the Cities*, from showing a conflict between two systems, or from didacticism. The audience is expected to participate in the growing conviction of Johanna and Pelagea Vlassova that violence is indispensable if injustice and oppression are to be resisted. Before he had read Marx, Brecht had probably joined the party committed to the idea of peaceful revolution; now, although never a member of the Communist Party, he came to share its Leninist commitment to violence.

In *The Mother* a large proportion of the dialogue is given over to explanation and instruction. In *The Threepenny Opera* there had been quite a lot of explaining. The songs comment on human behaviour, generalizing about endeavour, decency, sexual addiction and so on. Not that the characters who sing them have any expertise on these subjects. In this respect *St Joan of the Slaughterhouses* was a step forward. The explainers do give the impression of being qualified by specialist experience to discourse about the laws of supply and demand; what is unrealistic is that even the millionaire tycoon adduces economic arguments which transparently derive from Marx. In *The Mother* Brecht avoids this mistake by focusing on the process of learning, the mother receives instruction from her son, Pavel, a committed and hardened revolutionary.

During 1930, cataloguing in the notes to *Mahagonny* the contrasts between Epic Theatre and 'dramatic theatre', Brecht had reached for the word 'narrative', claiming that Epic Theatre moved away from the direct presentation of action. So it was advantageous to be working so soon afterwards on the adaptation of a novel. Instead of dramatizing it in the way that was – already in 1931 – all too familiar, Brecht let Pelagea Vlassova tell some of the story in monologue. When other characters (such as the schoolmaster) soliloquize, a second layer of theatrical reality is introduced, and the songs create a third.

Brecht shows enormous skill in grafting explanation and argument into the action and emotion. First the audience is invited to sympathize with Pelagea in her maternal disapproval of Pavel's political activities, which are dangerous. Why look for trouble? But when the Tsarist police, suspecting that a printing press is hidden in her home, brutally tear her furniture apart, our indignation is aroused on behalf of the innocent woman, who is having her scanty possessions damaged while being humiliated. She still has our sympathy when she offers, shortly afterwards, to distribute revolut-ionary pamphlets in a factory. This experience serves – both for her and for the audience – as a continuation of the learning process which is now gathering momentum. She sees how unjustly the workers are being treated. Like Johanna, she is being forced to confront experiences that will lead ineluctably to conversion.

Brecht's relationship with his mother had been a close one, and in the first draft of *Baal*, the son is not immune to the magnetism of her religious piety: he almost undergoes a change of heart. In the new play it is the mother who is converted: having been conditioned – partly through religion – to be submissive, she finally throws off the yoke. After Pavel has died as a martyr for the revolution, the neighbours piously visit Pelagea Vlassova to offer condolence, but she refuses to let them leave a Bible with her, and the holy book gets torn during an argument between the woman who owns it (she also owns the building) and a tenant who is about to be evicted. The property owner apparently loves her property more than she loves her neighbours, despite the injunction in the book she obviously values.

While the torn Bible conveniently symbolizes both the faith that Pelagea is rejecting and the contradiction between what the landlady professes to believe and the way she lives, Brecht was himself still strongly under the Bible's influence.

The stupid call him stupid, and the dirty call him dirty.
He is against dirt and against stupidity.
The exploiters call him a crime
But we know:
He puts an end to crime.
He is no folly, but
The end of folly.
He is no riddle
But the solution.
He is the simple
That is hard to achieve.

The syntax of this hymn in praise of Communism is unmistakably Biblical – Luther's German translation was almost contemporaneous with the King James version and has the same hard-edged simplicity, the same vitality and the same directness, allowing the paradoxes and the rhythmically balanced phrases to have their full effect. But it is not only Brecht's syntax that is Biblical: there are unacknowledged Christian elements in his Socialism. The assumption is that if all those who are heavy laden will go to Communism, its yoke will be easier, its burden lighter than the alternative yoke and burden.

THE SEVEN DEADLY SINS and
THE HORATIANS AND THE CURIATIANS

Die sieben Todsünden der Kleinbürger (The Seven Deadly Sins of the Petty Bourgeois) was written after Brecht, invited by Kurt Weill to write a scenario for a ballet which had been commissioned, insisted on incorporating songs.

The central idea was that two performers – a singer and a dancer – should represent different aspects of one girl. After arguing in *Man Is Man* that personality could be dismantled and reassembled, Brecht found different ways of splitting it. In *The Good Woman of Setzuan* he depicted a warm-hearted prostitute who, needing to defend herself against exploitation, disguised herself as a cold-hearted man; in *Herr Puntila and his Servant Matti*, Brecht introduced a land-owner who was generous when drunk and heartless when sober. In the ballet the dancer expresses the spontaneous, outgoing, unspoiled side of Anna's nature, while the singer is both narrator and an incarnation of disciplinary restraint, forcing her 'sister' to subordinate instinct to calculation, earning money instead of enjoying life. The seven sins are not really sins at all: it is merely in the interests of the bourgeoisie to inhibit healthy impulses.

As in *The Threepenny Opera*, prayer is used ironically. Anna's parents and her two brothers, intent on making her support them, pray for her to be granted the enlightenment that leads to prosperity. With her good looks she can probably earn enough to buy them a house. Idleness is the beginning of all vice, so it must be right that she should work hard. Pride is dangerous because she may want to dance like an artist: it is easier to please people and earn money by exhibiting her naked body. Anger is a sin – especially anger at injustice – because it may antagonize those who hold the purse-strings. Gluttony is dangerous because Anna's contract as a solo dancer in Philadelphia has a clause in it by which her weight must not exceed 110 pounds. Lust becomes problematic in Boston: she finds a lover who pays well but she prefers a gigolo, who takes money from her. Her 'small white bottom' is 'worth more than a small factory', so she must be careful how she invests it. And the family warns her against covetousness: if she asks for too much and gives too little in return, she will become unpopular. Envy, finally, is what Anna feels towards other people who can enjoy their lives without putting themselves on the market. But she perseveres for seven years, accumulating enough to buy a house for her parents and brothers.

Once again Brecht is using an American background to suggest that urban life corrodes rustic innocence – Anna comes from Louisiana. The implication is that industrialization makes it impossible for the two sides of the self to live in harmony with each other.

The next didactic play *Die Horatier und die Kuriatier (The Horatians and the Curiatians)* introduces a theme Brecht would develop in *The Roundheads and the Sharp-heads*. Like the kingdom of Yahoo, Curiatia is likely to be damaged by internal dissension arising from social inequality. So a strategy of distraction is adopted: warfare against the Horatians will unite the Curiatians.

Most of the play is written in blank verse, and, using a Chinese convention, Brecht makes one actor represent an army. With its superior equipment, the Curiatian army attacks the Horatian army. The Curiatian bowmen easily win the first battle, and the Curiatian lancers the second, but, as in so many Brecht plays, the outcome depends on cunning. In the third battle the Horatian swordsmen run away, but the Curiatian swordsmen, who pursue, are handicapped by their heavy armour. Separated from each other, the pursuers are defeated, so, in effect, 'The retreat was an advance.' One of Brecht's objects was to console all those (including himself) who had strategically retreated from Hitler's Germany.

THE ROUNDHEADS AND
THE SHARP-HEADS

Die Rundköpfe und die Spitzköpfe (The Roundheads and the Sharp-heads) is the first of Brecht's plays to deal directly with Hitler's rise to power, and the only one of them to be written inside Germany. In 1931, when Brecht started on the first version of the play, the Nazis were not yet in control and during the summer, not knowing how soon he would be a refugee, Brecht bought a country house. But the play contains impressive evidence of perspicacity.

The Roundheads and the Sharp-heads originated from an attempt to adapt Shakespeare's *Measure for Measure* for a group of young actors at the Volksbühne Theatre, Berlin, but the project fell through, partly because the adaptation deviated so far from the original. Shakespeare's Duke is made into a Viceroy who is also a landowner (as Hindenburg was), while Angelo is replaced by the Hitler-like Angelo Iberin, a ruthless fanatic, brought in to save the country from the crisis threatened when a left-wing organization known as the Sickle organizes the tenant farmers into resistance against the high rents.

There are two physical types in the country of Yahoo – the Tschuchen, who have round heads, and the Tschichen, whose heads are pointed. Angelo's racist policy of blaming all the country's maladies on the Tschichen mirrors Hitler's crystallization of prejudice against the Jews into a national policy. But Brecht was making the Party-line point that racism was a strategy designed to divert the people from the social conflict into which they ought to have been channeling their energy. The premiss is very similar to that of *The Horatians and the Curiatians*.

Iberin makes himself popular among the Tschuchen by intervening in a legal dispute between a roundheaded tenant farmer and his sharp-headed landlord, de Guzman, who is condemned to death. But de Guzman has a beautiful sister, Isabella, who, like Shakespeare's Isabella, wants to go into a convent, while Iberin, like Shakespeare's Angelo, is so obsessed with desire for her that he offers to spare the condemned man if she will go to bed with him. Brecht also borrows from Shakespeare the bed trick, by which the virgin's chastity is saved by means of substituting (under cover of darkness) the body of another woman who has already been the unscrupulous man's mistress.

Though Hitler was corrupt in many ways, he did not, apparently, have much difficulty in resisting sexual temptations; the common factors between Iberin and Hitler are their lower middle-class origin, their power as demagogues, their fanatical moralizing and their crafty confusion of racial and moral questions. Misdirection of judicial procedures was one of Brecht's favourite themes, and there is a fascinating lawcourt sequence when Iberin takes over from the Judge. The play also contains some highly effective street scenes parodying the activities of the ruffians in Nazi uniform who were already being given so much licence in German cities. In the play, the *Hutabschlager* (literally knockers-off of hats) are paid to go around the streets to find out whether hats are being used to conceal pointed heads.

As in *St Joan of the Slaughterhouses*, Brecht exerts himself to dramatize issues that concern the public as a whole. The naïve responsiveness of the German people to Hitler's racism is paralleled by Iberin's success in wooing the roundheaded tenant-farmers: he holds out the prospect that no more rent need ever be paid to sharp-headed landlords. This distracts the roundheaded tenant farmers from the need for solidarity with the sharp-headed tenant farmers against their common oppressors. These sequences are original and effective, though misleading as a diagnosis of what was happening in Germany. Brecht was uncritically following the simplistic Marxist assumption that international capitalism was fomenting anti-Semitism in Germany as a means of diverting energy from the class struggle, and that Hitler was no more than a tool in the hands of industrialist tycoons.

SEÑORA CARRAR'S RIFLES and FEAR AND SUFFERING OF THE THIRD REICH

The Roundheads and the Sharp-heads had evolved from a Shake-spearian adaptation into a play satirising a current political situation; *Die Gewehre der Frau Carrar (Señora Carrar's Rifles)* was intended from the moment of conception to influence reactions to a political event – the Spanish Civil War – but it is another variation on an unoriginal theme. J. M. Synge's one-act *Riders to the Sea* centres on a mother who loses her sons: having failed to keep the last of them away from the perils of life as a fisherman, she resigns herself to his death: 'No man at all can be living for ever, and we must be satisfied.' This stoicism was characteristic of the submissive fatalism that Brecht associated with tragedy, and he abominated it. He sets his play in the present, with the civil war as background. The mother is trying to dissuade both her sons from fighting, but, as in *St Joan of the Slaughterhouses* and in *The Mother*, the developing action converts the central female figure to radicalism and violence. Señora Carrar is so outraged by the death of her elder son that she not only encourages the younger to join in the fighting, she decides to join in herself.

Furcht und Elend des Dritten Reiches (Fear and Suffering of the Third Reich) consists of twenty-seven self-contained sequences showing how Nazism was affecting life in Germany. In Brecht's own words, the scenes constitute 'a catalogue of attitudes, the attitudes of keeping silent, looking over one's shoulder, feeling frightened etc. – behaviour in a dictatorship'.[1] To deal with current events, Brecht found himself, as in *Señora Carrar's Rifles*, adopting a more realistic style than usual. The scenes are like miniature one-act plays. He was in Denmark when he wrote 'Der Spitzel' ('The Informer') which is about a teacher and his wife who are terrified that their schoolboy son will denounce them for the anti-Nazi conversations he has overheard. Other scenes deal more directly with the perversion of judiciary power inside Germany. Judges were no longer free to deal justly with the cases they had to try. In one scene a harassed judge has to cope with a

1. *Arbeitsjournal*, 15 August 1938.

robbery in a Jewish shop. Another scene, set in a prison, shows that one baker is serving a sentence for mixing bran into his bread, while another, arrested a year later, is being punished for failing to mix bran into his bread – the Nazis had by then ruled that he should. Later, in *Mother Courage*, Brecht will show how a man is sentenced to death for continuing in peacetime with the behaviour that, in wartime, had won commendation from his superiors. In *Fear and Suffering* the state is shown to be unjust; in *Mother Courage* the point is that war makes immorality seem admirable. In both plays Brecht demonstrates his flair for dramatizing moral relativism.

Most of the scenes in *Fear and Suffering* concern the moral and practical dilemmas of middle-class intellectuals. In one sequence a Jewish wife, showing great discretion in choosing her words, says goodbye over the telephone to her friends. To stay with her non-Jewish husband would be to ruin his career; out of love for him she has decided to leave. She rehearses what she will say to him, but when he comes in, what she actually says is different. In *The Threepenny Opera* Brecht had made comedy out of moral paradox; here the paradox is in the historical actuality: Brecht is merely transcribing realistically, with pathos, but without comedy. Not that comedy is always lacking from these scenes, most of which dwell on absurdities that could not – except from a safe distance – be exposed as absurd. In one scene an embarrassed doctor has to describe injuries inflicted in a concentration camp. He takes refuge in the phrase 'professional malady'. In another a physicist has to manage without reference to Einstein who, as a Jew, is proscribed. Had Brecht written the play twenty years later, he might have introduced more comedy and more alienating stylization. His concern was journalistic: working from eye-witness accounts given to him by refugees, he was providing a dramatic summary of what was going on inside Germany. This does not mean that he was producing inferior art. Though the eyewitness accounts were second-hand, he succeeds (better than most other writers) in recreating the atmosphere engendered by the Nazi terror. He had, of course, one great advantage over the writers who had not run away: they did not dare to write about it.

THE LIFE OF GALILEO

Die Erde bewegt sich (The Earth is Moving) was Brecht's original title for the play that became *Leben des Galilei (The Life of Galileo)*. The subject attracted him partly because as a Marxist he believed that even cosmologies were propaganda for the prevailing social order; Galileo's world-picture was more democratic than the old Ptolemaic one, which put the earth at the centre of the universe, implying a rigid hierarchy, with God at the top and with Kings as his earthly representatives. Brecht's Galileo is not only a revolutionary scientist but a scientific revolutionary, full of relish for the subversive effect his teachings will have. Even the most powerful men in the world will come to seem less important and more peripheral: 'And the earth rolls gaily round the sun, and the fishwives, merchants, princes, cardinals and even the Pope roll round with it. The universe lost its centre overnight.' A cardinal may insist: 'I am walking on a fixed earth'; but stubbornness will merely make him look absurd, like King Canute giving orders to the tide. Man has lost his place at the top of God's priority list.

Unlike *The Roundheads and the Sharp-heads, Señora Carrar's Rifles* and *Fear and Suffering of the Third Reich*, *The Life of Galileo* was not written to counter current historical tendencies; apparently its main purpose was to secure the exiled playwright an entry visa to the United States. He had been told that the obstacles in the way of his entry might be overcome by a play – if an American company could be persuaded to produce it. Wanting to provide a meaty part – bait for an actor powerful enough to engineer a production – Brecht persuaded himself to write (just for once) about a famous historical figure; but there is no hero-worship in the play, and only the most perfunctory psychological and biographical interest in Galileo. Little of his private life comes into the picture: he is seen mainly as passive, a spar of wood carried forward by a powerful historical current.

In December 1938, just after Brecht had finished the play, it was announced that the uranium atom had been split, but apparently it was not until seven years later that he had doubts about the morality of pursuing scientific knowledge regardless of the outcome. At the beginning of 1938 he described the play as about 'Galileo's heroic struggle for his modern scientific conviction'.[1] Like Shaw's St Joan, who may have been a source of inspiration to Brecht, Galileo is a champion of the individual's right to think for oneself. But he is not heroic. Taking more pleasure than most men do in food and drink, he is also abnormally susceptible to intimidation when threatened with physical pain. Showing him the instruments of torture that the Inquisition has at its disposal is enough to make him abandon his intention of refusing to recant; like so many of Brecht's characters, he is determined to survive, and quite skilful in the art. Like Kragler in *Drums in the Night*, Galileo is undeterred by the prospect of having a reputation as a coward, but, unlike Kragler, he has an objective – one that can be attained by means of guile – a quality that figures frequently in Brecht's plays. And though he was in no position to write a guidebook on how to survive the Nazi reign of terror in Germany, he may have thought of the play as a message to intellectuals who were still living there: that guile was preferable to martyrdom. The 1938 version of *Galileo* contains an anecdote about a Cretan philosopher who for seven years submits to orders given by the man who has taken up residence in his house – the agent of a repressive regime. But the question 'Will you work for me?' is never answered until the agent dies. The philosopher can then afford to refuse. Like the Cretan, Galileo is not submitting as unreservedly as he appears to be. Despite surveillance, he writes his *Discorsi*.

'It accords with historical truth', said Brecht, 'that the Galileo of the play never turned directly against the Church.' In fact the historical Galileo maintained that scientific theory and theological dogma were concerned with different kinds of truth. It was only with difficulty that the Inquisition collected evidence against him, and it is possible that the injunction was a forgery. Cardinal Roberto Bellarmino, who appears in Brecht's play as Bellarmin, may have been responsible for this, but Brecht is not concerned to investigate the question. He wants to discredit the Church, but not through individual misdeeds. His object is to show that it is an oppressive force, used by the dominant class to preserve the existing situation. Even as a convinced Marxist, Brecht was never a conformist. He

1 *Berlinske Titende*, 6 January 1939.

never joined the Communist Party, and he enjoyed the sense of opposing all prevalent trends of thought. The only three command-ments he wanted to obey were: Thou shalt survive, Thou shalt work hard, and Thou shalt disagree. One of the questions he may have asked himself is how he would have survived the Inquisition if he had been inside Galileo's skin, and the answer is probably: in the same way that his Galileo does. Though excited by the possibility of discovering the truth through scientific research, he is not intoxicated to the point of risking martyrdom. Theatrically the obstinate obscurantism of the sixteenth-century Church is powerfully estab-lished by the scene in Florence, where a theologian, a mathematician and a philosopher from the court all refuse to look through the tele-scope. They trust their eyes when reading Aristotle but not when studying evidence which may conflict with authorized doctrine.

Brecht's image of himself as the Einstein of the new drama, may have helped him to identify with Galileo, and in spite of being so grudging with biographical information, he brings the character to vivid theatrical life, partly by means of letting self-portraiture filter into the characterization. In one of his working notes he wrote: 'As a confirmed materialist, he insists on physical pleasures. He wouldn't actually drink while he was working, but what matters is that he *works* in a sensual way.'[1] This was true of Brecht, as was Cardinal Barberini's comment on the scientist: 'He's more of a pleasure-fancier than any other man I've met. His thinking proceeds out of sensuality.'

Though Brecht's working routine was arduous, he welcomed inter-ruption, using visitors as an audience or even as collaborators, testing out ideas and pieces of dialogue, inviting suggestions and often incor-porating them in his work. He stimulated himself by stimulating other people, and from a remarkably early age succeeded in surrounding himself with disciples – friends who found he made them feel more alive, more creative. Galileo did not need friends capable of entering into a collaborative working relationship, but Brecht's Galileo is endowed with the same talent for attracting disciples. He works pleasurably in their company, instructs them – mainly by means of Socratic questions – and tests his arguments against their reactions. Their devotion to him is quite plausible, and it is put to good

1. *Gesammelte Werke*, vol XVII p. 1127.

theatrical use in the recantation scene. His daughter Virginia's hopes of marriage to an aristocrat have been wrecked by his truculent subversiveness, so she has turned to religion, and now she is praying for him to recant, but his friends are confident he will defy the threats of torture, and they are jubilant at the silence of the bells that would signal his submission to the authority of the Church. Belatedly these start to boom, and soon afterwards Galileo makes his entrance. According to the stage direction, he should be visibly transformed by his ordeal. He is just in time to overhear a remark of Andrea del Sarto's: 'Unhappy the land that has no heroes,' but he does not reply until after they have demonstrated the contempt they now feel for him. Eventually he says: 'Unhappy the land where heroes are needed.' In a just society, Brecht believed, unexceptional human qualities are sufficient. What is exceptional about Galileo – apart from his scientific genius – is not his courage but his guile. After writing the *Discorsi*, he succeeds at the end of the play in giving the work to Andrea when Virginia and a monk – both, in effect, gaolers – are out of the room. There is no tragic catharsis in this climax, but it does give the audience considerable satisfaction. 'Be careful when you go through Germany,' he tells Andrea, 'when you're smuggling the truth under your cloak.'

Brecht's original intention was that Galileo should justify himself by his success in outwitting his captors:

ANDREA: Together with the man in the street, we were saying: 'He'll die, but he'll never recant.' You came back: 'I've recanted, but I'll stay alive.' 'Your hands are dirty,' we said. You said: 'Better dirty than empty.'

GALILEO: Better dirty than empty. Sounds realistic. Sounds like me. New science, new morals.

But between the completion of the first draft in 1939 and the opening night of the first production in 1947, the splitting of the atom led to the use of the atomic bomb. 'Overnight,' wrote Brecht, in his Preamble to the American version, 'the biography of the founder of the new system of physics read differently.' Brecht now condemned 'Galileo's crime' as the ' "original sin" of modern natural sciences'. Galileo had done his duty to science but not to society. He had betrayed his belief in science as something that should improve the quality of life for the people. He had made the new astronomy into a 'sharply defined special science which – admittedly through its very "purity" i.e. its indifference to modes of production – was able to develop comparatively undisturbed'.

Wanting therefore to condemn Galileo without altering the play's structure, Brecht makes the character condemn himself:

> GALILEO: As a scientist I had a unique opportunity. In my lifetime astronomy reached the marketplace. In these quite special circumstances, the integrity of *one* man could have sent tremors all over the world. If I had held out, natural scientists would have been able to develop something like the Hippocratic oath that doctors take, a covenant to devote their knowledge exclusively to the good of mankind. As it is, the best we can hope for is a race of resourceful dwarfs who can be hired for anything. What is more, Sarti, I have come to the conclusion that I was never in real danger. For a few years I was just as strong as the authorities. And I surrendered my knowledge to those in power, for them to use it or misuse it, just as it suited them ... I have betrayed my profession. A man who does what I have done cannot be tolerated in the ranks of science.
>
> VIRGINIA: You have been admitted to the ranks of the faithful.
>
> GALILEO: Quite right. Now I must eat.

As in *Baal*, strong emphasis falls on naked greed for life, but this time moral judgements are not excluded. Unfortunately for the play, Brecht's lack of interest in the personalities of Galileo and his contemporaries encourages an overweighting of his historical significance. It is naïve to assume that by refusing to recant he could have set an example that would have had a lasting and decisive influence on the behaviour of future scientists. And one disadvantage of Brecht's dramatic method, in which each play is also an argument, is that fallacies in the argument are liable to cause flaws in the play, especially when he tries, as here, to change the main thrust of an argument without rewriting the play. His presentation of Galileo had gained more sympathy for the man, with all his failings, than could be reversed by giving him one speech of self-condemnation.

MOTHER COURAGE AND HER CHILDREN

Even if *Brecht* had not designed *Galileo* to secure himself an American visa, he would have felt guilty at writing what he considered to be partly an escapist play. In 1938, when it was easy to believe that one period of civilization was coming to an end, but almost impossible to believe a new one was beginning, he had been turning his attention to scientific discovery during the Renaissance. In *Mother Courage* he again moved back into the seventeenth century, but unlike *Galileo*, and like *Señora Carrar's Rifles*, the new play was written to make a direct impact on contemporary history. He could not seriously believe that it would impede Hitler's progress, but he assumed (as he nearly always needed to assume) that his work would not be entirely without effect. 'While writing I imagined that the playwright's admonitory voice would be audible in the theatres of various great cities, warning that if you sup with the devil, you need a long spoon.'[1]

He wrote the play within about three weeks, and it was easier to work fast if he could allow himself to draw freely both on his previous work and on other people's. He drew on Schiller's trilogy about Wallenstein's campaigns during the Thirty Years' War, on Hans Jakob von Grimmelshausen's novel *Der abenteuerliche Simplicissimus Teutsch* (*The Adventurous Simplicissimus Teutsch*) (1669), which was derived from the Spanish picaresque novel and based partly on confused personal experiences of fighting on both sides in the war. The name Courage is taken from Grimmelshausen's Landstörzerin Courasche, a beauty who first appears in the fifth book of *Simplicissimus*, where she is simply called Landstörzerin, but she reappears in the sequel, *Trutz Simplex: oder Ausführliche und wunderseltzame Lebensbeschreibung der Erzbetrügerin und Landstörzerin Courasche* (*Simplex Cussedness or Full and Wondrous Strange Account of the Life of the Arch-Deceiver and Female Rebel Courasche*). She acquires the name Courasche from her bravery in the battlefield, but the word

1. Brecht. 'Note for Scandinavian Audiences', cited by John Willett and Ralph Mann-heim in their Introduction to *Collected Plays* Volume 5, Part 2.

was also military slang for the female sexual organ. At first, through a series of marriages and love-affairs, she improves her situation, but then she contracts the pox and sinks into a life of crime. Brecht's Mother Courage also owes something to Lotte Svard, the attractive canteen woman in Johan Ludwig Runeberg's early nineteenth-century ballads about the Russo-Swedish war.

In one sense *Mother Courage* is a reworking of the main theme in *Señora Carrar's Rifles*. Courage tries to save the lives of her children, but she loses them, one by one, to the war, because she is financially dependent on it, selling drink, food, clothes and oddments to the soldiers. Believing that war was 'the continuation of business by other means', Brecht centres his action on a petty businesswoman whose trading activities revolve around the fighting. To her a peace treaty means that trade will be slacker. But her attitude to the fighting is not fundamentally different from that of people in more dignified and powerful positions. As she says, 'If you listen to the big shots, the war's being fought just from fear of God and for everything that's good and beautiful. But look closer and you see they're not so stupid as all that. They're in it for what they can get. Otherwise the small fry like me wouldn't go along with it.' Unlike Señora Carrar (or Johanna or Pelagea Vlassova), Courage does not undergo a conversion. This time the audience is intended to learn from the character's failure to learn.

Mother Courage is one of Brecht's best plays, partly because it draws more deeply and more fully than any since *Baal* on his gifts as a balladeer: it was in ballads that he could best express his keen lust for life. In *Galileo* there is one ballad which is performed in a scene that puts the Galileo story into a different perspective by showing how it might have been made into a subject for popular entertainment; in *Mother Courage* the whole play – more even than Brecht's ballad opera, *The Threepenny Opera* – is coloured with balladry. When Mother Courage and her children make their first entrance, they are halted by the sergeant and in answer to the question 'Who are you?' she sings her theme song. As in *Galileo*, and as in ballads, Brecht gives little biographical information about his characters, and even when they have names (Eilif, Kattrin, Peter Lamb, Yvette) or nicknames (Swiss Cheese) they remain, effectively, as anonymous as the types that appear in ballads or in Expressionist plays: the Brave Son, the Dumb Daughter, the Cook, the Honest Son, the Chaplain, the Prostitute, the General, the Sergeant and so on. Like Shakespeare's Falstaff, they are brought to robust theatrical life, but their vitality has nothing to do with individualization or with complexity. All the writing in the play is richly textured, and, like the dialogue in Shakespeare's history plays, it can make a realistic impression without being realistic. What the characters say has little to do with what their real-life equivalents might have said in similar circumstances. No less than the characters in *The Threepenny Opera*, the soldiers philosophize, alternately making points Brecht wants to make about the war and articulating attitudes to it that he wants to satirize, as when the sergeant condemns the anarchy that comes with peace or when the chaplain, insisting that the Lord will provide, finds pretexts for dilly-dallying.

In production, the play can be more effective than *Galileo* in creating the illusion that what we are seeing is more or less what we would have seen if we had been alive in the seventeenth-century and present at the scene, but whereas Galileo, though not a hero, was unquestionably a great man, Brecht tries in *Mother Courage* to give the impression that individual greatness is more or less irrelevant to historical events. This is not the history we find in books on the Thirty Years' War. Not only is the bulk of the action pitched very much lower down the social scale, it is pitched from a decisively anti-heroic angle. Like Mother Courage herself, the audience becomes more involved with the misadventures of the dumb daughter, who is assaulted and hit over the head, than with the death of Marshall Tilly, whose off-stage funeral occurs simultaneously. Asked whether the fighting will now stop, the Chaplain answers: 'Because the field marshall's dead? Don't be childish. There are dozens like that. You can always find heroes.'

Brecht is continuing the argument he started in *Galileo*: that in a reasonably good society, heroes would be unnecessary. In conversation with the Cook, Courage contends that only bad generals need heroic soldiers. Given good planning, ordinary qualities are sufficient. 'Whenever you find such great virtues lying around it always means there's something rotten . . . If a captain or a king is really stupid and leads his men into the shit, then they've got to be brave as hell, which is another virtue. Or if he's too mean and doesn't hire enough soldiers, then they've all got to be just like Hercules...In a decent country virtues aren't needed. Everybody can be perfectly ordinary, run of the mill, and, for all I care, cowards.' Here Brecht is making her talk in the style of the Good Soldier Schweyk.

Brecht had never made better practical use of his ideas about Epic Theatre than in writing *Mother Courage*. Admittedly his practice, like his theories, derived partly from the plays of Shakespeare and his contemporaries – plays in which the blank verse, the theatrical conventions, the stylization and the songs all function more or less like Brecht's alienation effects. But tragedy had since been domesticated, and though Strindberg and Ibsen were capable of breaking loose from Aristotle and the law of the three unities to write such plays as *To Damascus* and *Peer Gynt*, plays confined to a short time-span and to one or two indoor settings like *The Father* and *The Wild Duck* were more typical of their work and were easier to imitate. *Mother Courage* is impressive for its scale and sweep – ranging over twelve years and such a wide space – and for touching so tellingly on such a wide variety of human emotions. More than ever before, Brecht writes authoritatively and compassionately about the elemental sensations and emotions that might easily feature in a ballad – hunger, sexual desire, fear of death, maternal protectiveness, greed, vanity, anger at injustice, courage, military pride and so on.

Whereas Ibsen and Shaw had tended to ignore contradictions and anomalies within the self, Brecht was intent on breaking down the notion of consistency or coherence in the personality. Like Pirandello, he knew it was only in drama and fiction that characters always behave in a way that seems characteristic of them, and like Pirandello he was eager not to let audiences forget that they were in a theatre. But, unlike Pirandello, he had great influence. Mother Courage is shown to be capable of great loyalty to her children – she rejects the prospect of comfortable security in a Utrecht inn when the Cook, who has inherited it, refuses to let her bring her dumb daughter. But she is also capable of causing the death of her second son, Swiss Cheese, by haggling too long over the size of the bribe. She is generous enough to give away liquor when an old peasant woman collapses, but mean enough to be proprietorial about shirts when wounded soldiers are desperately in need of bandaging. It was Brecht's hope that these anomalies in her would make it easier for the audience to recognize that her behaviour was inconsistent and self-defeating, but an un-intended result of admitting so many contradictions into the char-acterization is that her individuality comes strongly into focus. We get to know her more intimately than any of Brecht's other characters, and we identify with her.

One of the reasons for his extraordinary success with her was that he was reaching through her towards two of his most neurotically sensitive areas – his hatred of trading and his memories of love between mother and child. Several of the play's most important sequences depend on friction between Courage's maternal instincts and her addiction to making profits, an evil which, unlike the evil ex-hibited to Joan in the Chicago slaughterhouses, is not based entirely on penury. She loses her brave son to the army when she makes the mistake of leaving him alone with the recruiter. In the first draft of the play she does this in order to give the sergeant a drink; in later drafts she is tricked into going round to the other side of the cart when the sergeant pretends to be interested in buying a belt. (Audiences had found her more sympathetic than Brecht intended her to be, and he tried, as he did in *Galileo*, to shift the balance of the play by making the central character seem more contemptible.)

Swiss Cheese is shot not because she cannot raise the ransom money, but because she is as addicted to bargaining as a gambler is to the game. At the same time, Brecht is determined to prove that trading is effectively murderous. This was a point he had made at much greater length in his 1934 adaptation of material from *The Threepenny Opera* into *The Threepenny Novel*. According to Peachum, the reason maimed (or apparently maimed) beggars are given so much charity is that the donors feel guilty at having inflicted the wounds. 'Whenever a man does business, isn't there another man somewhere else who's being ruined? Whenever a man supports his family, aren't there families elsewhere that are being forced into the gutter?' The novel denigrates the businessman as the criminal who is never brought to justice. Most people feel pleasantly exhilarated in market places, where they can approximate, buying or selling, to giving a theatrical performance, as they recommend a remedy for headaches or try on a headscarf. But Brecht had an almost pathological antipathy to trading. In the novel, Peachum becomes involved in selling unseaworthy ships to the Admiralty for use as troop-carriers in the Boer War. Since soldiers may be drowned when the ships sink, this particular business deal is, effectively, murderous, and to drive the point even further, Brecht develops the plot so that Peachum eventually has to choose between bankruptcy and arranging for the murder of the middleman in his dealings with the Admiralty. This does not prove that all trading is criminal, or that the pleasures of buying and selling are not as legitimate and almost as rudimentarily human as the pleasures of eating, drinking and making love. But in *Mother Courage* the daughter, like the two sons, is harmed by her mother's eagerness as a businesswoman. Kattrin would not have been assaulted if Courage had not sent her out on a business errand, and eventually Kattrin lets herself be martyred, drumming on a rooftop to awaken the Protestants in Halle when Catholic troops are trying to creep up under cover of darkness, but this episode could not have occurred if Courage had not gone off to buy goods in town, leaving Kattrin alone. Brecht's assumption was that if all property is theft, all trading is dealing in stolen goods; at one point Mother Courage does deal in stolen ammunition, exploiting the fact of its being stolen to offer a lower price. But perhaps Brecht was ambivalent in his hatred for trading: certainly he empathizes successfully with the woman in many contrasted business activities.

Undeniably, though, he is most successful of all in empathizing with her as a mother. Perhaps his mother was the only woman he ever loved. Apart from *Baal* and *In the Jungle of the Cities*, none of his plays draws directly on his relationship with her, but *Mother Courage* draws indirectly. Of the opportunities that the role offers an actress, two of the best are produced by the death of the second son. Both moments are silent. The first occurs when she hears the salvo of gunfire that kills him, the second when his corpse is brought in. To save her own life, she inhibits her natural reaction in order to convince the suspicious soldiers that it is the body of a man she does not recognize. A great playwright provides performers not just with words but with silences that show how they are driven to the limits of their endurance.

Emotion can be strongly expressed by the refusal to express emotion, and, as exploited by Helene Weigel in Brecht's production of the play, the two silences did not conflict with his ideas of Epic Theatre. The self-control on the actress's part was no less apparent than the self-control on the character's, and she was inviting the audience not only to sympathize ('Look what the poor woman has to endure just to stay alive') but also to criticize ('This is because she went on bargaining too long' and 'Look how hard she is').

Even in the revised version, though, we identify more than Brecht wants us to with Courage, and the continuous deterioration in her situation brings her sufferings closer to tragedy than he intended. At the end of the play, she has lost not only her three children, her man and most of her capital, but also her last hope of retiring from her arduous life on the road. She even has to pull the wagon herself now, instead of sitting in it while it is pulled by her children. In outlining the theory of Epic Theatre, Brecht had said that each scene was self-contained; here one leads to the next, as fortune's wheel inexorably pushes her downwards. Despite the undeniable effectiveness of the varied alienation devices, the tone is realistic, though sometimes the dialogue introduces imagery that smacks of surrealism. In the ninth scene we find Mother Courage reduced to begging outside a dilapidated parsonage, together with the Cook. The war is in its seventeenth year, and the winter in the Fichtelgebirge has been particularly harsh: 'In Saxony a man in rags wanted to give me a bundle of old books for two eggs, and in Württemberg they offered me a plough for a little bag of salt. Why go on ploughing? Nothing grows any more, only thorns. In Pomerania the villagers are supposed to be eating young children, and nuns have been caught carrying out highway robbery.'

Brecht owned two volumes of Pieter Brueghel reproductions, and it is possible that the pictures exerted an influence on imagery such as this. As in Shakespeare, the verbal images work closely in harmony with the stage picture. When the Queen in *Hamlet* describes the drowning of Ophelia, it is as if the picture created by the narrative is superimposed on the picture that the audience is looking at. In this Fichtelgebirge scene, an emblematic picture of starvation and wretchedness in Saxony is superimposed on the scene we see – hungry, ragged, desperate, ageing people, humbling themselves to beg.

Brecht's way of bringing history alive is comparable to Brueghel's – the human figures are not individualized in detail, but they come to life as individuals, and it is through their reactions to a big event that we experience it.

Mother Courage is also the most Shakespearian of Brecht's plays. In a 1941 diary he wrote:

> Plays like Shakespeare's Histories – chapters of chronicles, dramatised – have always struck me as the closest to reality. There is no 'idea' here, no plot is constructed, and it's scarcely topical. It's only an illumination of the well-established, with occasional corrections tending towards 'it could hardly have happened in any other way'. Courses on drama ought to begin with a comparison between, say, *King John* and the Chronicles it's presumably drawn from.

Much of Brecht's theorizing derives from his interest in Elizabethan drama; nowhere was his practice more healthily influenced by it than in *Mother Courage*.

THE TRIAL OF LUCULLUS

Brecht's radio play *Das Verhör des Lukullus* (*The Trial of Lucullus*) was based partly on a short story he had written, 'Die Trophaien des Lukullus' ('The Trophies of Lucullus'), while working on an anti-heroic Roman novel, *Die Geschäfte des Herrn Julius Caesar* (*The Business Affairs of Mr Julius Caesar*). In the story, the self-important general, confident that his fame will endure, questions the poet Lucretius about what it will rest on. Perhaps, the poet suggests, on his achievement in bringing the cherry tree to Europe.

What the radio play has in common with *Mother Courage* is a basic preoccupation with injustice in the distribution of death and suffering in war. It is the helpless majority that pays for the glory enjoyed by the leaders, who mostly take care not to put their own lives at risk. The action of the play is set in a heavenly lawcourt, where the general arrogantly expects to be honoured as he was on earth. But in charge of the case is a tribunal consisting of a peasant, a slave, a fishwife, a baker and a prostitute. They are used by Brecht as mouthpieces to express criteria which are equally remote from those of aristocratic Roman society and from those of conventional twentieth-century morality. Their sympathies are not with the leaders but with those who are led, not with the victorious but with their victims. Lucullus argues that the fishwife is in no position to pass judgement on him since she does not understand war. But the woman, who has lost her son in the battlefield, has no difficulty in convincing the court that she understands what war entails, and, reiterating the judgement Brecht had already passed in the short story, the tribunal finds that it can credit Lucullus with nothing but the introduction of the cherry tree. On the other hand, he is held responsible for 80,000 deaths. As the play ends, the court is withdrawing to consider what sentence to pass.

THE GOOD WOMAN OF SETZUAN

Prostitution is arguably the only trade in which the retailer is identical with the goods on sale. This point was basic to the play Brecht had started to write in 1930, calling it *Die Ware Liebe* (*Love as Commodity*). Wanting to separate selling from being saleable, a young prostitute begins to lead a double life, dressing in male clothes to run a tobacconist's shop, and changing into female clothes, which she can then remove in her other trade. During 1930, while he was living in Berlin, Brecht drafted five scenes, four of which still seemed usable when he resumed work on the play in Denmark during March 1939, and again, later in the year, after another move – to Sweden. He went on with the play until war broke out in September, putting it aside then until May 1940, when he was in Finland. Apart from *Man Is Man*, none of his plays had caused him so much trouble or had been abandoned and resumed so many times without the completion of a first draft.

In the first scene three gods are searching for one good human being – an opening which refracts Brecht's fear that human goodness would be in short supply after the war, while his sense of impending catastrophe finds its way into the mood prevalent in Setzuan, where 'Many people think that only the gods can save the situation.' It will soon become apparent that the gods are incapable of taking any init- iative – they are representatives of worn out values – but they are curious to discover whether goodness can survive in a world of penury and hardship. Atheists, says one of the gods (side-stepping the word 'Communists') are contending that the world must be changed because even the good people are finding it impossible to *remain* good.

In this play the good-hearted prostitute, Shen Te, is forced to divide herself, amoeba-like, into two halves, using a mask and male clothes to impersonate a cold-hearted protector, a cousin, Shui Ta. Without him she is helpless against the parasites and spongers who swoop down on her, after the gods – in gratitude for overnight accommod- ation – have given her money, which she has used to buy a tobacco shop. In *The Threepenny Opera* Brecht had made Mr Peachum express the view that everyone would prefer to be good, if only circumstances would allow it; in Shen Te we meet a woman whose inclination towards goodness is so strong that she would give away virtually everything she had unless she forced herself to start behaving ruthlessly. 'Being evil is like being clumsy,' she tells Yang Sun, the unemployed pilot. 'When we sing a song or construct a machine or plant rice, we're being generous.' To restrain her generosity is an effort, like holding her breath:

> To trample on fellow creatures
> Isn't it a strain? The vein in the forehead
> Swells with the effort of being greedy.

Brecht had made the same point in a short poem about a lacquered Japanese demon mask, which he kept on the wall in his study:

> Pityingly I see
> The forehead's swollen veins, showing
> The strain of being evil.

This view of human nature is optimistic and naïve, but it is cynically combined with an anti-romantic inversion of the disguise convention Shakespeare used in such joyfully optimistic comedies as *Twelfth Night* and *As You Like It*. In *As You Like It*, as in *The Good Woman of Setzuan*, it is corruption that forces the heroine into disguise, as if goodness cannot otherwise survive in a vicious world. Without the mask, Shen Te would have been unable to evict the homeless family of eight that arrives to camp in her new shop, and she would have been equally at the mercy of the landlady and the greedy tradesmen. In making her invent a relation whose personality contrasts with hers, Brecht is adapting the old comedy stratagem that had been used, for instance, by Oscar Wilde when he made John Worthing invent a convenient brother called Ernest.

When Shui Ta arranges for Shen Te to marry the barber Shu Fu, who is rich but unattractive and unpleasant, Brecht is using another stratagem that is common in comedy – setting up an undesirable suitor for the heroine as rival to the man she prefers. But there is nothing romantic about Brecht's treatment of Shen Te's relationship

with the unemployed pilot Yang Sun, whose interest in her turns out
to be not so much emotional or even sexual as financial. This hard fact
emerges in a scene which depends for its effect on the old theatrical
device of identity confusion. As in the sequences between Orlando
and the disguised Rosalind, the lover, who is talking about his girl,
fails to realize that he is also talking *to* her. What Orlando reveals is
how much she means to him; what Yang Sun reveals is how little.
Shen Te is willing to sell her shop in order to raise the money he needs
to bribe his way into a job as a pilot by getting another pilot sacked.
Although he has promised to marry her, he does not intend to take
her to Peking with him:

> SUN: I'm leaving the girl here. To start with she'd only get in my
>   way.
> SHUI TA: I understand.
> SUN: Why are you staring at me like that? You must cut your coat
>   according to the cloth.
> SHUI TA: And what's my cousin supposed to live on?
> SUN: Can't you look after her?
> SHUI TA: I'll see what I can do. (*Pause*) I'd like you to return the
>   200 silver dollars, Mr Yang Sun, and leave them with me till
>   you're in a position to show me two tickets to Peking.
> SUN: My dear cousin, I think you'd better mind your own
>   business.
> SHUI TA: Miss Shen Te . . .
> SUN: You can leave the girl to me.
> SHUI TA: . . . may no longer wish to sell her shop when she learns –
> SUN: Oh yes she will.
> SHUI TA: And you're not scared of what I'm going to tell her?
> SUN: My dear fellow!
> SHUI TA: You seem to forget she's a human being with a mind of
>   her own.
> SUN: (*amused*) I've always been amazed at the ideas people have
>   about their female relations and the difference a bit of straight
>   talk is going to make. Have you never heard about the power
>   of love or the itching of the flesh? You want to appeal to her in-
>   telligence? She hasn't got any intelligence. If I touch her on
>   the shoulder and say 'You're coming with me', she'll hear
>   bells and won't even recognise her own mother.

SHUI TA: (*wearily*) Mr Yang Sun.

SUN: Mr Whatever your name is.

SHUI TA: My cousin is obliged to you because . . .

SUN: Shall we say because I've got my hand on her tits? Stuff that in your pipe and smoke it.

The play ends in another lawcourt scene with the three gods as judges. In most of Brecht's lawcourt scenes the judge is unjust; in this one the judges are not unjust but ineffectual. In Brecht's godless world, there is no question of intervention from outside; this point is driven home to remind the audience that if the world is to be changed, human beings must themselves take the initiative. The gods have no solution to Shen Te's problem, no answers to the questions she raises in defending the action she took in inventing Shui Ta:

> goodness to other people
> And to myself were incompatible.
> To help both others and myself was too hard.
> Oh, your world is difficult. So much trouble and despair.
> The hand you hold out to the needy
> Gets bitten off. Those who help the lost
> Get lost themselves. So who can
> Refuse to become bad, when you can't live
> Without eating?

Brecht's intention is to leave the audience with the same feeling he tried to induce at the end of *St Joan of the Slaughterhouses*, that the important question is not whether we can be good, but whether we can take action towards leaving a better world behind us. He would probably have liked his own life to be judged according to this yardstick.

HERR PUNTILA and HIS SERVANT MATTI

In Finland Brecht stayed in Marlebäk in a small house on the estate of the writer Hella Wuolijoki. When he described *The Good Woman of Setzuan* to her, the dual character of Shen Te reminded her of the uncle she had used as model for her character Puntila in both the play and the sceenplay she had called *The Sawdust Princess*. During the 1920s, one of her uncle's escapades had caused a local scandal; like Shen Te, Puntila is two-sided – mean when sober and generous when drunk. On one intoxicated escapade in her play he acquires five fiancées, and he gives away banknotes. As a reward for helping him to get rid of the five women, his chauffeur is offered a marriage with Eva, Puntila's daughter. But, as in so many comedies from Menander to Wilde, the servant is not allowed to marry the girl until he has proved that, in origin, he is not socially her inferior.

In Brecht's view, social superiority was no guarantee of merit, and in his reworking of Hella Wuolijoki's story, he gives the chauffeur, Matti, a better claim on Eva than his rival, a junior diplomat: Matti is more of a man. When Puntila is drunk, this is clear to him; when he is sober, he is more intolerant: 'When I paid for you to have a good education in Brussels', he tells Eva, 'it wasn't for you to fling yourself at the chauffeur, but for you to keep your distance from the servants, or else they'll get bolshy and trample all over you.' In many conventional comedies, a birthmark or some other piece of evidence is uncovered to prove that the hero is socially more desirable than he had appeared, and will therefore be able to cross barriers he would otherwise have found insuperable; Brecht is more interested in demonstrating that class barriers can preclude the possibility of a happy ending. Instead of being united by a revelation, the lovers are compelled to acknowledge that the obstacles are too great: they have both been conditioned to stay in their fixed positions inside a hierarchical society. When they play a kind of charade in which Matti acts out the behaviour of an exhausted man coming home from work, Eva tries to demonstrate that she would be able to provide what he needs, but she fails despite her eagerness to obey his orders. Habituated to bourgeois politeness, she makes conversation when all he wants is to rest and read the newspaper. She is unskilled in darning socks. She shouts back abusively when his employer wants him to work in the middle of the night. In traditional comedies social inferiority was still being represented as a handicap: *Herr Puntila and His Servant Matti* is one of the first comedies to make social superiority into a handicap. Strindberg had written about the inept efforts of a well-born girl to please a servant lover and adapt her life-style to his, but *Miss Julie*, though not without its comic moments, is no comedy. Strindberg could never have relaxed sufficiently with this subject to write one.

There is common ground between *Herr Puntila* and Chekov's *The Cherry Orchard*. Brecht, while writing his play, was living on an estate which was comparable to Ranevskaya's both in typifying a declining aristocracy and in having reached the point at which its owner could no longer maintain it. Hella Wuolijoki, like Ranevskaya, was being forced to sell her property, while Matti, who understands machinery is, like Lopakhin, representative of a rising class. Puntila's failure to secure Matti as a son-in-law parallels Ranevskaya's failure to coax Lopakhin into a marriage with her adopted daughter Varya: the energies of the old ruling class are flagging, but it is incapable of forming an alliance with the rising class.

Once again the influence of Jaroslav Hašek's Schweyk is intrusive. Matti is at his best when he is using his humourous Schweykian native wit to persuade Puntila and Eva to take him seriously, and when he is ridding his master of the four fiancées – Brecht uses one less than Wuolijoki – but, although Matti shares with Puntila an imaginatively written scene in which they climb a mountain constructed out of chairs on a table, the character of Puntila, with its violent changes between drunken magnanimity and sober meanness, is theatrically better developed than the character of Matti, who loses sympathy towards the end as he rejects Eva, and, at the height of a drunken orgy, decides that the moment has come to leave his unpredictable employer.

THE RESISTIBLE RISE OF ARTURU UI

Brecht's main grievance against historians was that they treated the past as if it would have been impossible for events to turn out differently. The argument behind *Die aufhaltsame Aufstieg des Arturo Ui (The Resistible Rise of Arturo Ui)* was that Hitler's rise to power had not been unavoidable. If it had not been avoided, the fault lay with the people who could have resisted harder.

In equating Hitler with a Chicago gangster, Brecht wanted to show that, far from being a 'world-historical character' (to use Schopenhauer's phrase), Hitler was more passive than active, an unimpressive opportunist who let himself be carried along by social forces, like a feeble swimmer on powerful waves. *The Good Woman of Setzuan* and *Herr Puntila and His Servant Matti* had been anti-individualist in spotlighting a split in the central personality; the new play is anti-individualist in suggesting that Hitler's personality had little to do with his rise to power.

In *St Joan of the Slaughterhouses* Brecht had been trying to show that even tycoons were less influential than impersonal market forces; in *The Roundheads and the Sharp-heads* he had indicated that when an unhappy country needs a hero, it is less likely that a great one will emerge than that a mediocre one will be overrated. In *Arturo Ui* Brecht again sets his action in Chicago, but this time, with a gangster story to tell, he had no obvious alternative. Roma (Ernst Rohm) and his henchmen are murdered rather in the style of Al Capone's St Valentine's Day massacre, and Ui attends the funeral of Dullfeet (Engelbert Dollfuss, the Austrian Chancellor) just as Capone had gone to the funeral of a victim – O'Bannion.

Another element the play has in common with *St Joan of the Slaughterhouses* is the anti-heroic use of blank verse. To measure Ui against the heroes we associate with these rhythms is to look at him in an unflattering perspective. In a bookmaker's office he grumbles:

> The city has no money. Oh, short is the life
> Of local fame. No murder for two months
> And you're forgotten.

71

Later we are reminded of Mark Antony's 'Friends, Romans, country-men' rhetoric when a journalist pretends to sympathize with the mal-content gangster:

> And the loveliest scars
> Vanish with those who bear them. 'But can it be
> That in a world where good deeds go unnoticed
> No evidence remains of evil?' 'Yes.'
> 'Oh rotten world.'

The speech from *Julius Caesar* will be used again later when, wanting to discredit Hitler's oratory, Brecht shows Ui being tutored by a shabby tragedian. In reality Hitler succeeded in impressing millions of people; Brecht suggests that the effect depended less on personality than on a histrionic technique. References to Goethe's *Faust* and to Shakespeare's *Richard III* are introduced to imply that Hitler always calculates his effects. The garden scene from *Faust* is echoed in a flowershop scene, when Ui first makes advances to Betty Dullfeet, and at her husband's funeral, he tries to emulate Richard's success with Lady Anne. Literary parody is being used to make a point about contemporary history.

In *St Joan of the Slaughterhouses* Brecht had taken a great deal of trouble to dramatize the activities of the meat market. If in this play he takes relatively little trouble with the Cauliflower Trust, it is partly because he is writing allegorically about the Prussian Junkers. The German Chancellor, Hindenburg, had unwisely accepted a landed estate as a gift from them when they were pressing for government loans; in the play, the Mayor of Chicago, Dogsborough, who like Hindenburg is reputed to be incorruptible, buys a shipyard from the Cauliflower Trust at an abnormally low price. When Ui then offers him 'protection', he indignantly refuses, but at the official enquiry into the shipyard sale, a key witness is murdered, and the greengrocers are similarly terrorized into accepting Ui's offer of 'protection' after a warehouse has been burned at his orders. This parallels the burning of the Reichstag in 1933 when Hitler became Chancellor. The fire was almost certainly started by the Nazis, but the Communists were blamed. Four thousand of them were arrested, and Germany was intimidated into accepting a myth of law and order with uniformed thugs to impose it.

Brecht had a natural penchant for political allegory. Hitler's territorialism is represented by Ui's determination to extend his trading activities beyond Chicago, and his annexation of Austria is paralleled by the deal Ui finally clinches with Betty Dullfoot, who is director of a wholesale greengrocery in the small town of Cicero. The reference is to Dollfuss's ineffectual successor, Kurt von Schuschnigg, who tried to compromise with Hitler. At the Austrian election of March 1938, 98 per cent of the electorate voted for the Nazis: the reason for this is suggested in the play's final scene. At a meeting with the wholesalers from Chicago, the Ciceronean greengrocers are told that they are free to leave. No one, in fact, stops them from going, but the sound of machine-gun fire can only mean that those who leave are being shot outside.

THE VISIONS OF SIMONE MACHARD

Die Gesichte der Simone Machard (*The Visions of Simone Machard*) was the first play Brecht wrote in the United States, where he arrived in July 1941. It was completed early February 1942. As in *The Round-heads and the Sharp-heads*, he wanted to show that 'the Reich and the rich get on well together', but this time there was nothing oblique about his references to the Nazis, though he set the play in France and focused mainly on the attitude of the French towards their invaders. Once again it was the Joan of Arc theme that attracted him; once again he was choosing a female for a heroic role. He had been trying before Christmas to sketch out a play about a contemporary Joan who blows the embers of French patriotism into flaring against the Germans. At first he found it hard to make headway, but his friend Lion Feuchtwanger had been in France during 1940, and had been interned in Aix-en-Provence before escaping across the Pyrenees. Reading a draft of Feuchtwanger's memoir about his experience, Brecht considered it superior to any of his friend's novels, and it struck him that although twenty years had elapsed since their collaborative adaptation of Marlowe's *Edward II*, Feuchtwanger, with his first-hand experience of France during 1940, would be the ideal collaborator on the new play. In his diary Brecht complained that his friend's 'old-fashioned "biological" psychology delays us a bit', but gladly conceded that while they were constructing the action, Feucht-wanger's 'dogged defence of naturalistic probability' was 'really useful', though he 'wants nothing to do with anything technical or social (epic presentation, alienation effect, development of characters from social material instead of "biological", introduction of class conflicts into the story, etc.) and puts up with all that as just my personal style.'

As in '*The One Who Says Yes*', Brecht was determined to amputate all religious elements from the story, and as the German army advances, the voices heard by the young Frenchwoman, Simone Machard, are the voices of French working-class people, the black-smith and the peasants. Intent on remaining rich, the rich are willing to collaborate with the enemy; the poor are not.

The action is set during June 1940 in and around a hotel in a small French town on one of the main roads from Paris to the South. The hotel proprietor, who also owns a garage and a transport business, is being asked by the pusillanimous mayor to provide food for the retreating French soldiers and to lend his lorries to the refugees, who are desperate to escape before the Germans arrive. But the man is more interested in serving an elaborate meal to a captain who is obviously going to be a collaborationist. His name, Fétain, suggests Pétain.

Simone, who is working in the hotel, urges her boss to feed the refugees, and wanting to make sure that he will not hand his petrol over to the Germans she sets fire to it. In a series of dream sequences, she identifies with Joan of Arc, and the angelic voice she hears is apparently the voice of her brother, a soldier in the French army, who instructs her in resistance tactics. The play contains four dream sequences. The hotel proprietor and his devious mother are equated with the Connétable and Isabeau, the Queen Mother. The Mayor becomes Charles VII, while the captain, who also owns a vineyard, is the Duke of Burgundy.

Instead of martyrdom, Simone's punishment for her patriotic arson is confinement in an asylum run by brutal nuns. But the play ends optimistically. To show that actions like hers can be emulated, Brecht finally makes the sky redden: the refugees have set fire to the village hall.

THE DUCHESS OF MALFI and
SCHWEYK IN THE SECOND WORLD WAR

It was the actress Elisabeth Bergner and her producer husband, Paul Czinner, who commissioned Brecht to adapt Webster's play *The Duchess of Malfi* (1614). Needing a collaborator whose English was better than Feuchtwanger's, Brecht worked with H. R. Hays, who had translated both *Mother Courage* and *Arturo Ui*. According to Hays, 'I did all the writing, in the style of Webster, though Brecht and I discussed the scenes to be eliminated or added, and the content of scenes, and he sometimes contributed images.' Brecht wrote a good deal of new material in German, which Hays translated into blank verse.

Brecht was trying to improve Webster's play by tightening the construction and clarifying the motivation. Ferdinand is made to lust unambiguously for his sister's body, while the Cardinal's designs are on her property. Some lines from Webster's *The White Devil* (1612), were interpolated, together with a prologue based on the opening of John Ford's *'Tis Pity She's a Whore*, which was published in 1633 but staged earlier. Brecht cut the sub-plot involving Julia, the Cardinal's mistress, and it is the Duchess herself who in Brecht's version is murdered in the way that Webster's Julia is – she is made to kiss a poisoned prayer book.

In 1946, wanting to involve W. H. Auden in the project, partly for the sake of his name, Brecht alienated Hays, who withdrew. Auden thought Brecht was 'a most unpleasant man', one of the few people who deserved the death sentence. 'In fact I can imagine doing it to him myself.' They also disagreed violently about Webster's play, Brecht, as always in adaptations, wanting to make radical changes. He scaled down the role of Bosola, considering him to be no more than 'a librarian, a frustrated scholar,' and built up the importance of Delio, Antonio's friend. Antonio was the character that Auden wanted to play down: in his opinion the Duchess's relationship with him was no more than an escapade, but Brecht, who made both the Duchess and her brothers more class-conscious than they are in Webster, needed

Antonio because of his social inferiority. And Brecht rounded the play off by adding a scene in which Ferdinand kills the Cardinal.

As it turned out later, all the effort was wasted. Czinner and Bergner opted for the English director, George Rylands, whose Haymarket production, starring Peggy Ashcroft and John Gielgud, had been highly successful, and Rylands insisted on going back to Webster's original text.

It was only chance and Bergner that had drawn Brecht to Webster, but it was inevitable that sooner or later he would want to write a play based on an adaptation of Hašek's novel. Since working on the script for Piscator's production of *Schweyk* in 1927–28, he had been aware of its theatrical potential, and there had been strong Schweykian strains in several of his own characters, including Mother Courage and Matti.

In April 1943, attending an anti-Fascist rally, Brecht watched a show which included a comic sketch called 'Schweyk's Spirit Lives On', performed by two Czech actors. Like Brecht's *The Visions of Simone Machard*, the sketch was partly concerned with sabotage, and, shortly afterwards, simultaneous opportunities arose for a collaboration with Piscator on a new production of a Schweyk play and collaboration with Weill on a new Schweyk musical. It was typical of Brecht that he should want to pursue both possibilities simultaneously.

Rereading the novel in Grete Reiner's 1926 translation, he was

overwhelmed by Hašek's enormous panorama and the genuinely non-positive viewpoint of the people, which is itself the only positive, and therefore can't take a positive stand in relation to anything else. On no account must Schweyk become a shifty underhand saboteur. He's just opportunistic with the tiny opportunities that are left. He righteously upholds the existing order, which is so destructive for him, in so far as he supports any principle of order, even the nationalistic, which he encounters only as an oppressive force. His wisdom is subversive. His indestructibility makes him into an inexhaustible object of abuse and, at the same time, into the soil where liberation can grow.[1]

1. *Arbeitsjournal*, 27 May 1943.

This helps to explain why Hašek had got such a firm grip on Brecht's imagination: Schweyk was an individual incarnation of the non-individual. Unlike Pelagea Vlassova, Mother Courage and Shen Te, he was not someone who learned or failed to learn from experience of victimization; unlike Kattrin, Simone and Johanna he was not willing to risk martyrdom. Unlike any individual, he was immortal. He was the archetypal little man. He had guile (like Galileo) coupled with a subversive wisdom, which is apparent in the digressive stories he loves to tell, but his genius for survival puts him in line with Lindbergh's anonymous crew or the anonymous comrades in *The Remedial Action*, though the kind of dramatic narrative that Schweyk needs is much less stylized.

In his 'anti-Aristotelian' drama, Brecht had always assumed that it was misleading to put a hero on the stage as representative of a group. He believed that morality, law and conventional art were all weapons of oppression: the truth was to be expected only from the voice of the people. Anxious though he was to fight for social justice, to fight on behalf of the oppressed majority against the over-privileged few, he had often been outmanoeuvred by the stage's tendency to thrust personality into the foreground. Cinema is a more democratic art; in the theatre the audience tends to prefer those tough enough to thrust themselves forward, and Brecht had, as we have seen, enlisted more sympathy than he wanted for several of his more forceful characters, including Galileo and Mother Courage. In fact he called *Schweyk in the Second World War* 'a counter-play to *Mother Courage*'. The survival of the canteen woman implies that war will continue as long as there are profits to be made out of it; the survival of Schweyk implies that even war cannot destroy the people. Heroic drama had focused on leaders; the prologue to Brecht's Schweyk play is set in 'the higher regions', where a larger-than-life-size Hitler is asking for reassurance from his larger-than-life-size chiefs of staff: does the little man love him? The action that follows shows why the big leader has good reasons to be afraid of the little man.

Many of Brecht's characters had, like Kragler and Galileo, studiously avoided martyrdom, while several female characters, like Dumb Kattrin and Simone, had courted it. Schweyk almost magically combines the cheerfulness of the cynical survivor with the defiance of the heroic risk-taker. He discourages his fat friend Baloun from joining the well-fed German army, and to compensate him, provides the pub landlady, Anna Kopecka, with the slaughtered body of a stolen dog, so that she can cook a goulash. Schweyk saves her from the unwelcome attentions of a SS lieutenant, and then helps her to undermine the morale of a Gestapo officer by telling his fortune: she predicts death in the near future for him and for twenty men. Schweyk goes on to distract a sentry at a vital moment, with the result that a railway truck full of machine guns for Stalingrad is misrouted. He also saves a Russian family from a brutal Nazi padre.

Arguing that the Nazis were a more formidable enemy than the Austro-Hungarian Empire, Brecht claimed the right to counter-attack more sharply than Hašek had done, but in consequence his satire is crude, and Schweyk does not come so fully to life. He belongs to the Austrian Empire and to the First World War; no one could successfully have transposed him to the Second World War.

Brecht also got into trouble with the rights. He did not tell Piscator that he had started writing a text for Weill, but Piscator had secured the rights, and Weill lost some of his backers when they learned that there was likely to be litigation over copyright. The play was not finally produced until after Brecht's death.

THE CAUCASIAN CHALK CIRCLE

Like *Puntila*, *Der kaukasische Kreidekreis* (*The Caucasian Chalk Circle*) could be described as a fairy story for grown-ups. Outdoor scenes and natural images abound in both plays, and both deal with extremes of goodness and badness, leaving out the middle range of qualities. Both plays demand a production style which could not have been achieved at the time Brecht wrote them – he achieved it later, himself, in the Berliner Ensemble – and both are balladesque, but the ballad element in *The Caucasian Chalk Circle* is stronger; nothing in *Puntila* is stylistically comparable with the sequence when the narrator sings in verse the thoughts that Grusche cannot articulate.

Brecht's short story 'The Augsburg Chalk Circle', which was written in January 1940, shows that the Grusche story in the play has roots in *Mother Courage*. In the fifth scene of the 1939 play, Dumb Kattrin rescues a baby from a house where the roof could fall in at any moment. Rocking the baby, she makes inarticulate lullaby noises, ignoring Courage, who tells her to give the infant back to its mother. The sequence lasts for only two and a half pages, and the next episode, which occurs the following year, contains no reference to the baby or to Kattrin's frustrated maternal instinct, but in the story, which is also set during the Thirty Years' War, an Augsburg maid, rescues an abandoned baby from the house of a Protestant tanner, Zingli. For years she looks after it, and eventually, when the mother tries to reclaim it, the case is heard by the judge Ignaz Dollinger, 'who is famous throughout Swabia for his crudity and his wisdom'. He asks for a chalk circle to be drawn on the ground and for the child to be put inside it. The two women are then ordered to pull it out. The mistress at once succeeds because the maid cannot bear to hurt it, but the judge decides that it would be better off with her than with its mother.

The story derives partly from a judgement of King Solomon, who is said to have decided a similar case by offering to cut a disputed child in half and then awarding it to the woman who withdrew her claim. Another source was the thirteenth-century Chinese play *Chalk Circle* by Li Hsing Dao, which introduces the test of the circle, though the judge, who is the child's father, already knows who its mother is. In

80

1924 the playwright Klabund had made a German adaptation of this
play; both Brecht and Elisabeth Bergner were later to claim that they
had introduced him to the Chinese original in German translation:
Bergner in the book *Bewundert viel und viel gescholten: Unordent-
liche Erinnerungen* (Munich, 1978); Brecht in a conversation with
Luise Rainer in 1943. In the Solomon story and the play, the child is
awarded to its true mother; in Brecht's story and in his play, the
mother deserves to lose the child she has neglected, and it is given to
the woman who has proved herself willing and able to look after it.

Brecht started working on the play after Luise Rainer had told him
how much the role in Klabund's version appealed to her. A Broadway
backer, Jules Lowenthal, wanted to put on a show for her, and she
persuaded him to commission a new adaptation from Brecht, who was
paid an advance of $800.

Brueghel seems to have exerted an even stronger influence on this
play than on *Mother Courage*. Having tailored his adaptation of
Webster's play to Elisabeth Bergner, Brecht would not have thought it
unnatural to take the bearings for his new work of adaptation from the
beautiful Viennese star, who had arranged for him to be paid. But ten
days after sending her a script of the first version, he had misgivings
about Grusche. 'She should be artless, look like Brueghel's Dulle
Griet, a beast of burden. She should be stubborn instead of rebel-
lious, placid instead of good, dogged instead of incorruptible, etc.,
etc.'[1] And he glued reproductions of Dulle Griet to the title pages of
the first copies. As he put it, the Brueghel painting shows 'the Fury
defending her pathetic household goods with the sword. The world at
the end of its tether.' *The Caucasian Chalk Circle* shows a world at the
end of its tether, and the characteristics of the Fury are divided
between Grusche and the Governor's selfish wife, who abandons her
baby son until it becomes financially advantageous to reclaim him.

As in *Mother Courage*, the influence of Brueghel was pulling
Brecht in the same direction as his own instincts – those of a balladeer.
Unlike the subject–matter he had used in *Mother Courage*, his
material in the new play could not have been treated naturalistically.
His villainous rulers, his merciless soldiers, his greedy peasants, his
cowardly policeman and his eccentric judge are characters who might
have stepped out of a fairy tale or ballad, but he also brings big areas

1. *Arbeitsjournal*, 15 June 1944.

of human experience into focus as he modulates between stylized action and poetic narration.

One index of the play's quality is the richness of its dramatic texture. The story-telling is vigorous, the language muscular. In some ways this is closer than *Mother Courage* was to Shakespearian drama. The History plays are not the model this time. When Grusche and her lover talk across an imaginary stream or when she, to save the baby from the pursuing soldiers, has to walk across a frail and swaying bridge over a precipice, we are closer to *King Lear* and to the intensity of the demands it makes on an audience's imagination. These are scenes Brueghel might have depicted; another is the peasant wedding with a big cluster of neighbours gathered tightly around the bed of a man who, to avoid enlistment, pretends to be dying. It was partly from Brueghel, but also partly from observation that Brecht had learnt how ugly elements could be incorporated into a beautiful stage picture. He had also learnt something from Brueghel about the value of hinting that the patterns of human idiocy are as unchanging as the pattern of the seasons.

At the same time as having second thoughts about Grusche and wanting to make her less virtuous, Brecht was having second thoughts about his other main character. Azdak is a more obviously Brechtian creation than she is – a ribald, drunken Schweyk, elevated to the role of judge, so that once again, as in *The Exception and the Rule*, *The Roundheads and the Sharp-heads* and *Fear and Suffering of the Third Reich*, Brecht would have a yardstick for measuring the corruption of justice. This time justice would be done, but almost accidentally:

> First I had only his lousy jurisdiction, which made poor people come off well. I knew I mustn't suggest that the normal laws should be bent for justice to prevail, but to indicate that with careless, ignorant, even bad jurisdiction, something emerges for those who really needed law. That's why Azdak had to have the self-seeking, amoral, parasitical features of the lowest, most degenerate of judges. But I still needed an elementary cause of a social kind. I found it in his disappointment that with the overthrow of the old masters, what ensued was not a new era but an era of new masters. So he goes on enforcing bourgeois law, only dilapidated, sabotaged, adapted to serve the unqualified self-interest of the judicature.[1]

1. *Arbeitsjournal*, 8 May 1944.

The justice he dispenses is exceedingly rough. He solicits and receives bribes, even if they have no influence on his verdicts. When an innkeeper accuses a stableman of assaulting his daughter-in-law, Azdak condemns the girl for assaulting the man. 'Do you think you can go around with hindquarters like those and get away with it in court? This is premeditated assault with a dangerous weapon.' He confiscates a dun-coloured horse he has always fancied, and orders Ludowika to go out with him to the stable, 'so that the court can investigate the scene of the crime'. Afterwards, dealing simultaneously with the dispute over the child and with a divorce pending between an old couple after fifty years of marriage, Azdak, like the judge in Brecht's short story, applies the chalk circle test, awarding the child to the maid, while, affecting absent-mindedness, he divorces not the old couple but Grusche and the man she has married to provide a home for the baby – the man who had avoided enlistment by pretending to be on his deathbed. Grusche is now free to marry her lover, and Brecht has deftly fused the Azdak story with the Grusche story.

What is less satisfactory is the stylistic disunity between this double section of the play and the more naturalistic opening in which delegates from two Kolchos villages, including a tractor-driver and an agronomist, are arguing about the ownership of a Caucasian valley. The play-within-the-play is not performed in order to settle the argument: the representatives of the goat-herding Kolchos have already surrendered their claim in favour of their fruit-growing rivals, who offer the play as an entertainment. Thematically there is a connection between the prologue and the play: the principle

> That what there is should belong to those who are good for it,
> Children to the motherly, so that they thrive,
> Carts to good drivers, so that they are well driven,
> And the valley to the irrigators, so that it bears fruit.

When the play is driving towards this point, it is perverse to cut the prologue, as many directors do, but the stylistic shift is awkward, and the ostensibly realistic beginning is unconvincing. People with a legal claim to a valley do not surrender as willingly as the goat-herds do: Brecht did not seriously believe or seriously expect his audience to believe that disputes were settled like this in Stalin's Russia. He is idealizing and romanticizing no less than in the two stories that follow, but these are devoid of sentimentality – partly because there is plentiful evidence of greed and cruelty, partly because he had the right second thoughts about Grusche and Azdak.

The Caucasian Chalk Circle reprises many themes Brecht had handled in earlier plays. In *Mother Courage* the characters had to change their image, their values and their life-style when war gave way to peace, though none did so as funnily as Jussup, the peasant who pretends to be dying until the danger of enlistment has passed.

In *Drums in the Night*, a soldier returned from a war to find his girl pregnant by another man; here Simon Shashava returns to find Grusche with a child and married. The comedy and the neat dramatic trick which removes the obstacle to the lovers' reunion would have been beyond Brecht's powers when he wrote *Drums in the Night*.

In one sequence Grusche attempts to pass herself off as a well-born lady when, wanting shelter for the child, she spends the night at an inn in the company of noble refugees. Here Brecht is inverting the substance of the sequence in *Puntila* when Eva tries to prove her downward social mobility. Both girls fail: in Brecht's view the social hurdles can be removed only by revolution.

The final scene in *The Threepenny Opera*, when the arrival of a royal pardon saves Macheath from the gallows, is echoed in a sequence at the beginning of the Azdak section. Screaming, he is being dragged to the gallows by soldiers who suddenly release him. Another familiar element is the satire on law courts, while the explicit insistence that laws should be re-examined to see whether they are still valid is reminiscent of the boy's attitude in *The One Who Says No*: why not reconsider the old customs and preserve only the ones which are good? There is, finally, also a counterpart in *The Caucasian Chalk Circle* to the sequence in *Galileo* which shows how Cardinal Barberini's attitude changes as he is dressed in the Papal vestments: Azdak has the line: 'It would be easier for a judge's robe and hat to pass sentence than for a man without all that.'

Though none of these arguments is new in Brecht's work, he had never advanced them in such a relaxed way. Of all his plays *The Caucasian Chalk Circle* is his most joyful celebration of being alive.

THE DAYS OF THE COMMUNE and TURANDOT OR THE CONGRESS OF WHITEWASHERS

If we discount a 1947 adaptation of Sophocles's *Antigone*, (taken largely from Hölderlin's version), Brecht allowed five years – longer than ever before – to elapse without writing a new play. When the war ended in 1945 he had a tremendous stockpile of unproduced work, and it is understandable that his main ambition, as soon as Germany and Austria were freed from Nazism, was to arrange productions for these plays. He felt that a play was not even finished until it had been staged. The years 1945–9 saw the premieres of *The Caucasian Chalk Circle* and *Puntila*, besides giving Brecht his first opportunities to watch productions of *Galileo* and *Mother Courage*. *The Good Woman of Setzuan* had been premiered in Switzerland in 1943, and it was revived in Vienna during 1946, but Brecht who was still in America until 1947, saw neither production.

More important, though, than any of these premieres was the creation of what was effectively his own company, the Berliner Ensemble, at the beginning of 1949. Belatedly, at the age of fifty, he was, like Shakespeare and Molière, a playwright with his own company. It was only now that an adequate production style was evolved for such adult fairy-tales as *Puntila* and *The Caucasian Chalk Circle*, while *Galileo*, *Mother Courage*, *The Good Woman of Setzuan*, *The Mother* and other important Brecht plays were staged superbly and distinctively in a style that was to influence the development of the theatre – and even the cinema – all over the world. But, unlike Shakespeare and Molière, Brecht did not benefit substantially from the opportunity of writing with particular actors in mind. Between 1949 and his death in 1956 he wrote only two plays, which are not among his best. *Die Tage der Commune* (*The Days of the Commune*) and *Turandot oder Der Kongress der Weisswäscher* (*Turandot or the Congress of Whitewashers*).

Like so many of Brecht's plays from *Baal* onwards, *The Days of the*

Commune evolved out of vehement disagreement with another play-wright's work. *Nederlaget* (*The Defeat*) was a play about the Paris commune of 1871, written in 1933 by the Norwegian Communist Nordahl Grieg. It had been translated into German by Brecht's friend Margarete Steffin, who had died in 1941, and he had possibly collaborated on her version. He began thinking about it again while he was looking for a play to open the Berliner Ensemble's first season, and Piscator was invited to direct it for him. In March 1949 when Brecht started adapting it together with Neher and Ruth Berlau, he was still hoping that Piscator would say yes, but as the hope faded, the adaptation became more free. *The Days of the Commune* is not a counter-play to *Nederlaget* in the same sense that *Baal* is a counter-play to Johst's *Der Einsame*, but where Grieg criticized the Commune for lacking effective leadership, Brecht praised it as a spontaneous uprising. The Central Committee called on citizens to elect 'men of the people', and in Brecht's opinion, they were responsible representatives of the popular will.

As in *The Caucasian Chalk Circle*, he reprises several themes from earlier plays. He was attracted (as he had been in *Galileo*) by moments when it was possible to believe a new age was dawning, but here this theme is treated ironically. He had suggested in *Simone Machard* that true patriotism could be expected only of the working class: the bourgeoisie should be expected to align itself with the enemy in order to prevent property and wealth from being redistributed; at a meeting of the National Guard's Central Committee in *The Days of the Commune*, Varlin says: 'Now go and fetch Herr von Bismarck, so that he can protect your property from those who made it, the proletariat.'

All Brecht's previous plays centre on an individual, but *The Days of the Commune* centres on a group of neighbours. The play divides its focus almost equally between a workman and his mother, a school-mistress and a seamstress, a baker and his brother, a student priest. We also get glimpses of Bismarck and Thiers, while several scenes are set in the Commune, where delegates are making speeches. In fact, Brecht was approximating more closely than ever before to the kind of play Piscator had presented in the 1920s: perhaps the idea was to launch the Berliner Ensemble with a true ensemble play.

The dialogue sometimes lapses into slogans and clichés, but there is enormous vitality in the writing. Brecht researched the subject thoroughly, reading Marx's pamphlets, the Commune's *Journal officiel*, Hermann Drucker's collection of documents and Prosper Lissagaray's eyewitness account of the events. Brecht may also have been influenced by Büchner's play *Dantons Tod* (*Danton's Death*), which he was simultaneously considering for the Ensemble. But to some extent *The Days of the Commune* was an argument against *Danton's Death*. Büchner had focused on a hero who refused to act; Brecht was widening his focus to take in a group which heroically refused to act violently. In his view Danton 'betrayed the revolution because he hobnobbed with the aristocracy, protected it, admired it, let it admire him, generally becomes a star, etc. Is therefore responsible for the Terror which was necessary (necessary against him) a Terror which then swallows up Robespierre too.'[1]

For Brecht the brief period of the Commune's supremacy was like a golden age of democracy in which rational discussion could lead to enlightened decision. He succeeds here where he failed in the Prologue to *The Caucasian Chalk Circle* – in giving the impression that this is happening. For once, power is in the hands of reasonable revolutionaries – too reasonable, in Brecht's opinion, in the sense of depending too much on reason without violence. Fair-minded and moderate, the leaders restrain the mob from marching to Versailles and unseating the government of Thiers, and from using force to take money from the bank. Unlike Johanna in *St. Joan of the Slaughterhouses*, unlike Pelagea Vlassova, unlike Señora Carrar, the Communards are not converted to violence: they therefore die on the barricades, while Thiers and a group of bourgeois citizens watch from a safe distance.

Turandot oder der Kongress der Weisswäscher (*Turandot or the Congress of Whitewashers*) was Brecht's last play, written in the summer of 1953, after the abortive rising of 17 June, in which he had sided with the East German government against the insurrectionary building workers. Overstrained by arduous norms, which were suddenly raised, while their wages were arbitrarily cut, the workers marched in protest to the government building and held a mass meeting in the street. The rising was no less spontaneous than that of

1. Letter to Helene Weigel, 6 September 1949, in *Briefe*, Frankfurt 1981.

the Paris Commune, but Brecht knew that an official decision was shortly to be taken about the future of the Theater am Schiffbauerdamm, which had been promised to the Berliner Ensemble. It could not have been a worse moment for him to take the risk of antagonising the government, and he gave it his full support against the rebels.

The whitewashers in his play are the Western intellectuals who write apologias for capitalism, but he must have known that his satire would be taken in the West as equally applicable to intellectuals in the East. In fact the play may originate partly from guilt feelings about his failure to protest when Soviet tanks fired on workers.

One of the play's main subjects is the difference between good lying and bad lying. The perverted princess is sensually aroused by good lying, while suitors who lie badly are beheaded – which approximates more closely to the fate that overtakes Eastern dissidents than that of their Western counterparts. During the 1930s, Brecht had been intending to write a play about Turandot, and what he did now was combine some of his ideas for it with material he had accumulated for a satirical novel about intellectuals, or Tuis, as he called them. In 1934 he had been thinking of setting the action partly in China. In the play, the characteristic of the Tuis is that they live by selling the produce of their brains. 'In our day their brains feed them better when they hatch out something that harms a great many people.'

Brecht had always hated intellectuals: part of his enthusiasm for sport had negative roots in his hostility to intellectuality. In the play, the emperor's brother, who is creating an artificial shortage by keeping cotton off the market, asks him: 'What do you have your 200,000 whitewashers for?' It is during a sequence set in the school for Tuis that the play touches most directly on the issue which had provoked the rising. The teacher, Nu Shan, is instructing his pupil, Shi Meh, by manipulating a pulley which raises a breadbasket whenever Shi Meh is in error, lowering it when he is correct. He is trying to answer the question: 'Why is Kai Ho in the wrong?' Kai Ho is a Marx-like redeemer who never appears on stage.

> Kai Ho speaks of liberty. *The basket moves*. But in reality he wants to enslave the ferrymen, cottagers and weavers. *The basket sinks*. It is said that the ferrymen, cottagers and weavers do not

earn enough – *the basket rises* – for their families – for them to live in luxury and over-abundance with their families – *the basket sinks* – and that they have to work too hard – *the basket rises again* – for they want to spend their lives in idleness – *the basket stays still* – which is indeed natural. *The basket moves.* The dissatisfaction of many people – *the basket stays still* – is exploited by Kai Ho, who is therefore an exploiter. *The basket sinks rapidly.*

THEORIES and PRACTICE

It is sometimes contended that Brecht was at his best as a playwright when he paid least attention to his own theories of drama, but this is a gross simplification of a complex and constantly changing relationship between practice and theories: there is no single Brechtian 'theory' – there is a pragmatic succession of theories. Like any playwright, he began to form ideas about theatre before he began to write plays; like many modernist playwrights, he started by writing a form of anti-theatre, activated less by any positive idea of what theatre should be than by forceful opposition to current practice. At first his ideas about theatre were formulated only in conversations, letters, diaries, note-books. By the time the formulations had hardened into dogmas, he had behind him considerable experience of writing and directing.

In the first version of *Baal* (1918) the poet-hero, working temporar-ily as a theatre critic, produces a scurrilously dismissive review of Schiller's *Don Carlos*. The following year, when Brecht was working temporarily as a theatre critic for the left-wing paper *Der Volkswille*, he compared *Don Carlos* unfavourably with Upton Sinclair's novel *The Jungle*: Schiller's play, being less relevant to current social and economic problems, was inferior. Not that Brecht, at this stage, was interested in politics; if he attacked the idea of private ownership or defended the Communists during mealtime conversations, it was mainly to annoy his father.

He was disinclined to concern himself with psychological analysis or with quirks of individual character, but this was more a matter of temperament than of conviction. It was on differences between one personality and another that previous writers of novels and plays had centred their work, but Brecht was instinctively an anti-conformist. He did not want to write plays like Hauptmann's, with their 'rather stupid precision in delineating people';[1] nor did he want to repeat a mistake most historians made: ignoring such questions as 'what the Pope ate and drank, how he loved, what his clothes and his servants were like, whether he washed and how often, and what his smoking

1. *Tagebücher*, 6 October 1921.

90

habits were! And there's no history of fashion in dress, crafts, trading or the social position of merchants, soldiers, priests.'[1]

Brecht's distaste for empathy dates from this early period. He prided himself on his restraint in *Baal* and *In the Jungle of the Cities*: he had not interfered with the 'splendid isolation' of the audience, or invited identification with the hero. 'There's a higher kind of interest; in making comparisons, in recognizing what is dissimilar, incomprehensible, inexplicable.'[2] Writers of tragedy were too nervous either to side with nature against the hero or to make fun of nature, 'to mimic the repulsive mooing of the stupid cow that has swallowed the grasshopper'.[3] Ibsen, like Hauptmann, had been too compassionate: 'The stalls are taught to be "understanding" about everything.'[4] The audience was obliged to take the same view of the characters as the playwright did; Brecht wanted to hold back and let people make up their minds for themselves.

Combined as it was with his first opportunity to direct a generously budgeted production, Brecht's collaboration with Lion Feuchtwanger on the adaptation of Marlowe's *Edward II* helped to crystallize his ideas about how to deviate from the stylistic norms. His production assistant, Asja Lacis, had been in the Soviet Union, and she may have been the filter through which certain ideas characteristic of Meyerhold and Vakhtangov penetrated into his work. In her autobiography she claims to have originated the device of giving the soldiers immobile, expressionless faces and making them march like marionettes.[5] The idea of giving them clown-like make-up was suggested by Brecht's friend, the comedian Karl Valentin, who was sitting in on some of the rehearsals. So Brecht began to use alienation effects long before the phrase occurred to him, and he was already demanding an acting style that was cool, clear, devoid of rhetorical emotionality. He also insisted on realism in performing actions that would be familiar to the characters. Soldiers, for instance, would have developed a casual expertise in putting nooses around necks.

1. Ibid., 26 October 1921.
2. Ibid., 10 February 1922.
3. Ibid., 11 February 1922.
4. Ibid., 16 November 1921.
5. Asja Lacis, *Revolutionär in Beruf*, ed. H. Brenner, Munich 1971.

The central assumption in his play *Man Is Man* (1924) – that a human being is a machine which can be dismantled and reassembled – was an idea that had been latent in the work of Fernand Léger and Marcel Duchamp, who had both been brutal in their use of the machine analogy to make statements about the human body, while in Germany *die neue Sachlichkeit* (the New Objectivity) was jerking fashion away from beauty and emotionalism towards functionalism. Brecht was quite willing to make terms with the ugly, the streamlined, the functional, the interchangeable: 'After enjoying black coffee I can look more tolerantly at concrete buildings... I believe: surface has a great future... I'm glad that in cabarets dancing girls are being manufactured to resemble each other more. It's pleasant that there are so many of them, and that they're interchangeable.'[2]

Implacably hostile to the self-intoxication and the exclamatory emotionalism of the Expressionists, he aimed to contribute constructively to contemporary society. Posterity was of no consequence: the artist should be a clear-thinking worker in the collectivist society. Turning away from traditional culture, Brecht tried to align his art with mass entertainment. Bored or irritated by current theatrical styles and techniques, he sat with pleasure at sporting events. Unlike the theatrical audience, the sporting audience knew exactly what to expect: 'that trained people display their particular skills in the manner most suited to them, with the finest sense of responsibility, but in such a way as to give the impression that they're doing it for their own enjoyment.'[2] 'Objective' was the word Brecht used to describe the technique of his favourite boxer, the heavyweight champion, Samson-Körner. A new theatre was needed in which individual style was discarded, and in which actors and spectators both knew exactly what was required of them.

In 1924, when Erwin Piscator directed *Fahnen* (*Flags*), which was described by the author, Alfons Pacquet, as an 'epic drama', Brecht's friend Alfred Döblin, the novelist, called it 'a stepping-stone between narrative and drama'. This form could always offer refuge, he added, when 'the coldness of a writer's feelings stops him from identifying

1. *Autobiographische Aufzeichnungen*, p.205.
2. *Scriften zum Theater*, pp 61–2.

with the characters' fates or the story's development'.[1] This is in line with Brecht's belief that the audience should not be told what to think of the characters.

Elisabeth Hauptmann noted on 23 March 1926: 'Brecht finds the formula for epic theatre – play from memory (quoting from gesture and posture)'. He was now orienting his writing entirely to this. In July, a couple of months before the premiere of *Man Is Man*, he told an interviewer that his plays were 'objective' – independent of his private moods. They reflected the mood of the whole world: 'Today the meaning of a play is usually blurred because the actor aims straight at the audience's hearts. The characters are presented ingratiatingly, and therefore falsified . . . they ought to be put across quite coldly, objectively and classically. They're not subjects for empathy: they are there to be understood. Emotion is private and blinkered; understanding is reliable and comparatively wide-ranging.'[2]

When Brecht started to read Karl Marx at the end of 1926, one of the effects was to harden his antipathy towards the bourgeoisie and towards the individual, and in 1927, when he had to judge a poetry competition, he made usefulness his criterion, and awarded the prize to a piece of doggerel about a cyclist. The poem had not even been entered for the competition.

Working as a member of Piscator's dramaturgical collective, Brecht was probably influenced by what he saw in rehearsal. Determined to communicate with a new, unsophisticated audience, Piscator was experimenting to find ways of shifting the focus away from the individual. Wanting to inflame the desire for social change, he studied the Soviet example, and presented contemporary history panoramically. In the interests of objectivity, he used detached commentators and cinematic projections, and sometimes, to highlight the gap between the subjective and the objective, he introduced a contrast or counterpoint between live actors and screen images. But because he was less dependent than Brecht on words, it was easier for Piscator to be consistent in his hostility to both traditional theatre and theatrical tradition.

If Brecht was also hostile to the theatrical and rhetorical tricks which

1. *Leipziger Tageblatt* 5 June 1924.
2. Interview with Bernard Guillemin in *Die Literarische Welt*.

could blunt the audience's critical faculties, this may have been partly because he was watching Germany's failure to resist the rise of Hitler, who was better than any actor at arousing his audiences to hysteria. The quality Brecht admired in acting was restraint. When Helene Weigel played the maid (or the second messenger) in *Oedipus*, Brecht praised her in print for calling out ' "Jocasta is dead" without any grief, but so firmly and irresistibly that at this moment the naked fact of her death had more effect than any private pain could have evoked. Her style was at the opposite extreme from that of actors who "put themselves and the audience into a trance".'[1] Instead of encouraging the audience to recognize how bizarre it is that a character behaves in this or that way, they invite sympathy or even empathy. Brecht rejected theatrical magic. In the poem 'On Everyday Theatre' (1930), he argues that actors should learn from 'the theatre which is played on the street'.[2] The woman from next door imitates the landlord; men show giggling girls how, ostensibly resisting, they show off their breasts. With a crowd of passers-by as tribunal, a man describes a street accident, imitating now the old man who was run over, now the man at the steering wheel. Without implying that the accident was unavoidable, and without pretending to be either of them, he demonstrates what they did. Nor does he mind being interrupted: he can answer questions and then resume his performance.

Brecht developed his ideas about epic theatre in the notes he wrote during 1930 on *Mahagonny*. His intention, he said, had been that 'some irrationality, unreality and frivolity should be introduced in the right places to assert a double meaning'.[3] This would discourage empathy. Instead of feeding the spectator with sensations and reducing his capacity for action, Epic Theatre demanded decisions from him and tried to stimulate his capacity for action. Dramatic theatre implied that human nature could not be changed: Epic Theatre assumed not only that it could, but that it was already changing. Weill had already made the point, apropos *The Three-penny Opera*, that a realistic plot forced him to make the music work against it: either the plot was interrupted to give space to the music or

1. *Schriften zum Theater*, I, p. 211.
2. 'On Everyday Theatre', *Collected Poems*, p. 176.
3. *Versuche* 2.

'brought to a point where there was no alternative but to sing'.[1] Weill's theorizing also anticipated that of the eclectic Brecht in using the term 'Gestus' to mean both gesture and gist. In his notes on *Mahagonny* Brecht said that everything in the opera had been based on the gestural: 'the eye which searches for the gestural component in everything is morality.'

While Brecht's theories derived primarily from practice, there was a powerful counter-current. His 1931 production of his 1924 play *Man Is Man* was quite different from any staging he could have visualized in 1924, when he had not yet been exposed to the influence of Japanese Kabuki theatre. Using masks, padding and stilts for the soldiers, he was simultaneously dehumanizing the characters and stylizing the play with alienation effects. Though he was no longer holding back from telling the audience what to think, he was partly compensating for that with violent anti-illusionism.

Temperamentally he had always been allergic to tragedy, with its implication that individuals are powerless to fight off a catastrophe or to deflect fate from its pre-ordained course; by the beginning of the 1930s he had become politically committed to demonstrating that neither human nature nor the social environment was unchangeable. In aiming to make drama less dramatic and more narrative, in opting for the kind of action to which suspense is only intermittently important, he was making the story-line discontinuous, creating gaps to show that the will-power of the characters could have been asserted to make events go one way rather than another. His lawcourt scenes, besides encouraging the audience to take sides, serve as a reminder that human judgement can be decisive.

In 1935, when Brecht was in Moscow, he saw a Chinese company led by the actor Mei Lan Fan, who used no make-up or costume or lighting changes, and never concealed his awareness of the audience's presence. To Brecht he appeared to be quoting – not imitating. Brecht's use of the word *Verfremdung* (alienation) dates from this performance. In his native dialect, Bavarian, the words *Verfremden* and *Entfremden* are synonymous, and previously he had used *Entfremdung* to mean the defamiliarization which is necessary to stop a familiar event from seeming natural or readily acceptable. In art it is always

1. Weill, *Ausgewählte Schriften*, 1975, p. 54.

desirable to strip away some of the familiarity that stops the observer from responding attentively to a familiar object or action, but in Brecht's work the defamiliarization was aimed primarily at making the spectator look critically at human behaviour and question whether the events under observation were avoidable. Nothing should be exempt from the question: is this necessary?

Mei Lan Fan could indicate passion without feigning the loss of self-control. Instead of registering anger by breathing heavily or raising his voice or tensing his neck muscles, he would chew at a lock of his own hair. In his ability to play a character without immersing himself in it, he reminded Brecht of Chaplin. Brecht's essay 'On the Alienation Effects in Chinese Acting'[1] shows that the influence of Mei Lan Fan on his ideas was comparable to that of the Balinese dancers on Artaud in 1931 before he formulated his ideas about Theatre of Cruelty. To both Brecht and Artaud it seemed as though the dominant Western cultural tradition was more superficial, more frivolous than the Asiatic.

Throughout Brecht's sixteen years of exile from the German-speaking theatre, theorizing was a compensatory pleasure. Without seeing his scripts translated into three-dimensionality on the stage, he could only visualize and generalize, legislating for the theatrical future. The essay 'The Street Scene', written in 1938, develops the analogy he had used eight years earlier in the poem 'On Everyday Theatre'. Like the witness, who is partly describing, partly re-enacting what he saw, the actor (according to Brecht) should neither reproduce emotion nor induce it as if it had intrinsic value. Theatrical performance, like the street-corner demonstration, should have a social objective: it should either help to expose attitudes that tend to cause accidents, or it should establish who on this occasion was to blame. The acting of the eyewitness is not illusionistic: no one will identify him with either of the drivers.

Most people would probably pick a street-market as providing better examples of histrionic behaviour in a public place, but Brecht disliked the *raison d'être* of markets, while an accident was the ideal event to support him in his long-running battle against the notion of inevitability.

1. *Brecht on Theatre*, p. 91.

It was not only his analogies that were conditioned by personal taste and political opportunism. His theories were tailored to his needs of the moment. 'Our concept of realism needs to be broad and political', he insisted in 1938, when he was trying to counter Lukács's assumptions about realism. Brecht went on to propose five principles: that realist art should expose the network of causes operating on society, and should show the dominant viewpoint to be that of the dominant class, but the artist's viewpoint it reflects should be that of the class which has proposed the broadest solutions for the most urgent social problems: though it should encourage abstraction, art should be concrete, and it should focus on the dynamic of growth.

No longer in competition with Piscator, Brecht could afford to be more generous, and in a lecture on experimental theatre he gave in 1939, he paid tribute to Piscator for treating the audience like a legislative body – inviting it to make decisions on the basis of evidence submitted by means of images, statistics, slogans, historical facts. Previous playwrights and directors had tried to weld the audience into a unified reaction, but politically a play would be more educational if it split the audience into two hostile sections.

Brecht's longest theoretical dissertation, his *Short Organum for the Theatre* (*Kleines Organon für das Theater*)[1] was written in Zürich during 1948. It was modelled on Francis Bacon's *Novum Organum* (1620), which had been directed against Aristotle's *Organum*, and had argued that all learning should be based not on theory but on experiment. Making the assumption he had made in *Galileo*, Brecht contended that science and its by-product industrialism could have evolved in a way which would have benefited humanity more if only scientists had been less greedy for the money they could make by passing their discoveries on to the men who would exploit them commercially.

Though ambivalent in his attitude to science, Brecht was excited by its achievements, and he argued that the 'scientific age' needed a new kind of theatre. Drama had never shaken itself free from its tragic concern with relationships between men and gods. Since art and science should both be dedicated to making human life easier, theatre

1. *Brecht on Theatre*, p. 179.

should provide 'workable representations of society which are then able to influence society'.[1]

He had not been using the term 'alienation effect' until 1935, but, in the *Organum*, he claimed that 'the variety of acting which was tried out between the first and second world wars at the Schiffbauerdamm Theater in Berlin was based on the alienation effect', and he defined the function of alienation as making an object recognizable but unfamiliar. The audience should be helped to stop looking at social circumstances as if there were no alternative to them, and to develop that critical stance 'with which the great Galileo observed a swinging chandelier. He puzzled about this swinging as if he had not expected it and failed to understand it. In this way he arrived at the laws which were operative.'[2] To discover the laws of motion that governed society, each historical situation should be considered as part of a process – examined in terms of its anomalies.[3] Tragedy, from *Oedipus* to *King Lear*, had dealt neither with variations in human nature nor with internal contradictions. Because it was concerned only with the meeting ground between human and non-human forces, it assumed that human nature never changed. Epic Theatre should show that it did, shunning the over-simplification of making actions fit character and character fit actions.[4] It should bring into focus not only the areas of disharmony or contradictions between the character and his behaviour, but also those between the actor and his performance. In the American production of *Galileo*, Charles Laughton had appeared 'on the stage as a dual figure, as Laughton and as Galileo'.[5] The actor would have been incapable of disappearing totally into the part; nor would the audience have wanted him to:[6] it was partly in order to see Charles Laughton that people were buying tickets.

On 9 January 1948, Brecht had copied into his diary a passage from one of Goethe's letters to Schiller:

The dramatic plot moves before me; around the epic I myself

1. *Brecht on Theatre, Little Organum*, Section 24.
2. Ibid., Section 48.
3. Ibid., Section 45.
4. Ibid., Section 52.
5. Ibid., Section 49.
6. loc. cit.

move while it seems to stand still . . . If the event moves before me, then I am bound fast to the sensual event, my imagination loses all freedom . . . I am pulled by an external force. If I move around the event . . . I can vary my pace . . can step backwards or forwards. This fits in very well with the idea of the past, which can be conceived as static, and with the idea of *narrative*, for the narrator already knows the end when he is at the beginning or in the middle, and consequently each moment is of equal value to him, and so he maintains a quiet freedom throughout.[1]

Brecht was under the influence of this analysis when he demanded in his *Organum* that the actor should be a narrator – should maintain a quiet freedom and share it with the audience. He should be under no obligation to give the impression that everything is happening for the first time.[2] If he empathized with his character in rehearsal, he should not do so in performance.[3] He should not try to magnetize the audience's attention all the time he is on stage: moments of respite should provide breathing space for critical thoughts.[4] And when working on a role the actor should memorize not just his lines but his initial reactions to them – objections, surprise, criticisms – so that something of these can be incorporated into the performance, like annotations.[5]

Brecht was making an important formulation of principles that run counter to Stanislavski's. With his high moral standards, his insistence on empathy, and his tendency to make the actor think in terms of the character's 'super-objective' or long-term motivation, Stanislavski, especially in the earlier phases of his career, would often smooth out inconsistencies and anomalies. He would neither let the actor contradict the character nor the character appear inconsistent. But people are inconsistent. Brecht's attitude was more realistic: 'The coherence of a character will in fact materialise out of contradictions between his individual qualities.'[6]

Even if Brecht had not gone on to create the Berliner Ensemble, he

1. 26 December 1797.
2. *Little Organum*, Section 50.
3. Ibid., Section 53.
4. Ibid., Section 49.
5. Ibid., Section 57.
6. Ibid., Section 53.

would, in the *Organum*, have struck some valuable blows against 'the current theatrical abuse of letting the leading actor, the star, "steal the limelight" by making all the other actors subservient to him: he makes his character formidable or wise by forcing his partners to make theirs frightened or attentive'.[1] Though he was not always objective as an observer of relationships between masters and servants, bosses and employees, Brecht understood that two-way traffic is involved in all power structures, and he made a democratic proposal he would later put to good practical use: 'in rehearsal actors should exchange roles with their partners so that the characters get from each other what they need from each other . . . The master is only the kind of master that his servant allows him to be.'[2] This suggestion has since proved useful, and not only to directors who have committed themselves to political positions like Brecht's. But just as Stanislavski had insisted that the precondition for good acting was moral goodness, Brecht insists that the precondition is Socialism: 'If the actor does not want to be a parrot or an ape, he must familiarise himself with today's knowledge of human relationships by joining in the class war . . . No man can rise above the warring classes, for no man can stand above the human race.'[3].

Today it is impossible to speak with any confidence about the relationship between Stanislavski's theories and his practical achievements as a director; to those who saw them before Brecht died in 1956, his productions were unforgettable, and though he was never strait-jacketed by his own theories, there can be no doubt that they were of value to him. They were never discussed in rehearsal, and most of his actors had not read his theoretical works, but Brecht had benefited from the depth of thought which the theorizing had necessitated. Reacting in practice, as he had in theory, against the stodgy rhetorical declamation which was prevalent on the German stage, he encouraged actors to rehearse in their native dialect. This induced relaxation and increased expressiveness. Stage German was 'only a feeble shorthand without overtones or undertones. People themselves speak

1. Ibid., Section 59.
2. Ibid., Section 59.
3. Ibid., Section 55.

this language as if it were foreign.'[1] And he immediately found it advantageous when he introduced alienation effects into rehearsals: they clarified the turning points in the action, while actors could be prevented from identifying with their characters in the traditional way. Instead of merely speaking their lines in rehearsal, they were sometimes asked to interpolate the words 'he said' or 'Courage said'. This forced them into a position more like that of a narrator. At the same time it helped in subordinating psychological considerations to social ones. As a director, Brecht was always anxious to avoid psychological or analytical arguments. 'Don't tell me,' he would say, 'show me.'[2] During the two hundred hours spent on rehearsing his adaptation of Lenz's play *Der Hofmeister* (*The Tutor*) only fifteen minutes, it was calculated, were spent on discussion.

One phrase which often recurred in Berliner Ensemble rehearsals was: 'It should be demonstrated that . . . '[3] The object was not so much to tell a story about particular individuals in a particular set of circumstances as to state a case about a social situation. Brecht was interested in making historical statements. In his hands each play became a piece of history that was also relevant to the present, and whereas most directors, in instructing an actress on how to handle a pot of lard, for instance, would be concerned primarily with characterization and theatrical effectiveness, Brecht was likely to be more concerned with the plight of those who live close to starvation, and with their reverential attitude towards food. He also believed that it should be possible to tell virtually the whole story of a play through actions, so that even an audience of deaf people would have been able to understand what was going on. At the Berliner Ensemble, after the dress rehearsals, he would always hold a 'marking' rehearsal. Speaking their lines quickly and perfunctorily, the actors had to go through the whole play, preserving movements, rhythm and pauses.[4]

Impelled partly by his natural perversity, he struck a series of damaging blows against clichés in casting and characterization. Why

1. *Arbeitsjournal*, 5 March 1950.
2. *Theaterarbeit*, p. 131.
3. Michael Mellinger, 'Goodbye to Berlin', *Encore*, No. 27, September-October 1960.
4. Carl Weber, 'Brecht as Director', *Tulane Drama Review*, Autumn 1967.

should all princes be princely, all statesmen stately?[1] Instead of characterizing superficially according to type, he insisted that everyone had a heterogeneous mixture of temperamental traits, and that directors could help actors to develop by casting them in roles to which they might at first have seemed unsuited: these roles would expose the qualities they normally concealed. At the same time, casting against type might help to highlight contradictory inclinations in the character. 'The actor should cultivate all temperamental elements, for his characters come to life only through their own contradictoriness.'[2]

It might seem possible to distinguish between Brecht's achievement as a playwright, his achievement as a theorist and his achievement as a director, but the influence he is still exerting proceeds from all three areas of activity. He was not the first German writer who tried to make theatre more political. Hauptmann's *Vor Sonnenaufgang* (*Before Sunrise*, 1889) had centred on the attempts of a socialist agitator to help a group of oppressed Silesian coal miners. *Die Weber* (*The Weavers*, published 1892, produced 1893) was innovative in giving a proletarian twist to bourgeois domestic tragedy and in wrenching the action away from personal relationships and individual predicaments. The focus of the play is not on a hero or a representative family but on a rebellion. Hauptmann even used the word 'epic' apropos his attempts to put dramatic action in a social and political perspective. 'The modern dramatist,' he wrote in August 1912, 'being a biologist, may sometimes work towards a drama which, like a house, an architectural creation, never moves from the position where it has been situated. Or he may have reason to apprehend life horizontally, having already grasped it vertically. He may prefer life's *epic flow* to its *dramatic stasis*.' *The Weavers* is a prototypical example of the historicizing theatre that Brecht developed, but unlike Hauptmann, Brecht was a canny enough practitioner to develop the full potential of his artistic programme. He was a successful artistic revolutionary.

1. *Messingkauf Dialogues*, Fourth Night.
2. Ibid.